*For all workers and reflective practitioners who make lives
better for all working people.*

# WORKING
# STORIES

## Essays by Reflective Practitioners

### Edited by
### ED MURPHY

### WDI PRESS
Albany, New York

# CONTENTS

## Acknowledgments

Thanks to the many people who worked hard to publish this anthology: Donna Gaetano, project manager; Esther Cohen, bookdoctor; Ilana Masad, copy editor; Laura Tolkow, designer; Cindy Hochman, proofreader; and Fort Orange Press, printer.

**Thank you to the writers, who are reflective practitioners all.**

# WORKING STORIES

# FOREWORD

Mario Cilento

In this unique anthology developed by the Workforce Development Institute (WDI), union leaders, activists, and members from around New York State share their thoughts through essays about the successes and struggles of working New Yorkers.

With passion and conviction, clarity and truth, they explain why their work matters.

This compelling collection of stories explores the critical role the labor movement plays in the lives of working men and women, and their families.

The organized labor movement is the single most important entity toward ensuring a better life for working men and women, both during their work years and in retirement.

Better wages, benefits, and conditions of employment for union members are easily identifiable and well documented. Whether it's more money in your paycheck or safer working conditions, the advantages speak for themselves.

The facts and figures to prove the value of union membership have rarely been disputed. Rather, and unfortunately, they are routinely ignored by those who want to see the labor movement diminished, or worse, eliminated.

And that gets to the heart of the matter of what the labor movement is up against in this country. Today, labor's opponents and adversaries don't only want to beat us, they don't only want to defeat us; they literally want to eliminate us. Their best day would be if they woke up tomorrow morning and the labor movement didn't exist. In addition, they are better funded and better coordinated than ever before. We need only look at the fact that there are now 25 so-called right-to-work states in this country. And the assault is ongoing.

Here in New York State, we have noted countless times that we are never going to have the ability to outspend our opponents. Historically, the way we have been able to fight back, level the playing field, and win more often than not, because we still win more often than not in New York, has been as a result of our ability and willingness to join together on issues of shared concern and interest.

When we stand together, join together, fight together, and raise our voices together; (public sector, private sector, and building trades); we win. Working men and women win and future generations win. Because, collectively, we have the power and ability to raise the standard of living and quality of life of all working people.

But that only happens when we make the most of who we are as a movement. We represent 2.5 million members in New York. We have 3,000 local affiliates of the New York State AFL-CIO, and 24.8 percent of the workforce is organized in our state. But those numbers don't mean much unless we are all coordinated, working off of the same page, working out of the same playbook. When we share strategies, messaging, and best practices, we are able to further the cause of all workers.

In the last few years, we have secured historic legislative victories, such as raising the maximum unemployment insurance benefit, and indexing it. We have raised the minimum Workers' Compensation benefit. And we have won the battle on safe patient handling legislation, which will exponentially improve worker safety and health in hospitals, nursing homes, and healthcare facilities throughout the state.

So there are victories to build upon; victories born of collective effort and intensity.

But we are fighting for so much more. We are fighting for a better today and brighter tomorrow for all workers and their families.

While the facts, figures, and victories are all verifiable, sometimes it is the practical realities and examples of a better life that inspire us toward collective action.

What follows is my personal experience of what it is that we are fighting for, every single day, collectively as a labor movement.

Throughout my childhood, my father was a very active union member. He was a rank-and-file member of Local #3 of the IBEW. He was never elected to office in his union. He was sort of the ultimate union volunteer. He would do anything to help his union. He'd volunteer for legislative campaigns, political campaigns, picket lines. You name it, he was there. He was eventually asked to coordinate the New York City Central Labor Council's Labor Day Parade. As a volunteer, it meant that he would put in a full day's work and then set out to coordinate the largest Labor Day Parade in the country.

When I was growing up, from time to time my father would try to explain to my sister and me why he wanted to give something back to his union, and this movement.

We would sit around the dinner table at night and he'd say things like, "I want to give something back to my union, because my union isn't just about me, it's about my family. And my union isn't just about the present, it's about the future." That was very difficult for a 10- or 12-year-old child to comprehend, but we heard it many times throughout our teenage years.

When I became a union member myself in 1990, I thought I had a better grasp on what he meant. And, in fact, I did understand the basic concept much better than I had as a teenager.

But I found that I first truly started to understand what my father meant, in practical terms, unfortunately, when he passed away suddenly at the age of 55. When I lost my father, even though he was still a relatively young man, he left my mother a sizable pension, as well as several annuity funds. He had been putting money away in those funds for 35 years as a union member.

Between my father's pension, my mother's smaller pension, and eventually my father's Social Security, my mother was able to spend her retirement years the way we would all hope to live them. With dignity, with self-respect, and independence. She never had to ask either my sister or me for a dime.

She was able to do all the things you'd want to do when you retire. She could go to dinner or the movies with her friends, and she could spoil her five grandchildren. She would spoil them with Christmas presents, birthday presents, and presents for the sake of presents.

I was starting to see exactly what my father meant when he said "my union isn't just about me, it's about my family. It's not just about the present, it's about the future."

However, it wasn't until two years ago when I really, truly, got the full picture of what my father meant all those years earlier.

Two years ago, my mother passed away, and when she did, my sister and I each received a letter from my father's union.

We were told that we were the beneficiaries of what was left in my father's annuity funds. We were surprised and thankful.

After reading through the letter, my wife and I had a discussion about what we would do with the money. While it wasn't a life-altering sum, it was just enough that we had to decide what we would do with the small windfall. We decided that since this was unexpected, and since we have three daughters who will hopefully someday go to college, we would put the money in the bank for their education.

On the day that I received the first check of several installments, I went to the bank to make the initial deposit. I remember going to the bank, depositing the check, and taking the receipt from the teller.

And then it hit me. As I walked out of the bank and got into my car, I finally understood his words from 30-some-odd years ago.

My father became a union member sometime around 1965. My oldest daughter's first year of college will be 2021. 1965 to 2021, that's 56 years.

So, more than a half century after my father first became a union member, my father will help to pay, in some small way, for my daughter, his granddaughter, to attend her freshman year of college.

A granddaughter, mind you, WHOM HE NEVER MET.

I can still hear the words "my union isn't just about me, it's about my family. It's not just about the present, it's about the future."

My father could not have known all those years ago how his life would work out. And what lay ahead. But he knew in his heart that by being a union member, he was part of something greater than himself. That he was part of a movement that was committed to providing a better life and greater opportunities, not just for the member, but for future generations of workers and their families.

That is what we are fighting for every day as a movement.

We fight for a better today and a brighter tomorrow for all working men and women, and their families.

We have to secure an American Dream that promises the next generation will do a little bit better than the generation before it. That the next generation will be a bit more financially secure than the generation before it. And that the next generation will have a brighter future than the generation before it.

That's what this movement is all about.

And it brings us back to the basic tenets of unity and solidarity.

When we stand together, and join together, and fight together, and raise our voices together, then, collectively, we can deliver that American Dream to our members, their families, and generations to come.

**Mario Cilento**
*President, New York State AFL-CIO*
*August 20, 2015*

# WORKING STORIES

# INTRODUCTION
## We Learn From Each Other

Ed Murphy

*Two roads diverged in a yellow wood ...*

*I shall be telling this with a sigh*
*Somewhere ages and ages hence:*
*Two roads diverged in a wood, and I —*
*I took the one less traveled by,*
*And that has made all the difference.*
— "The Road Not Taken," Robert Frost

Through stories, we learn from elders, teach our children, share with each other, grieve, celebrate victories, admit mistakes, and move through defeats to start over. I am Irish. I don't sing or play music, but I do talk, and have kissed the Blarney Stone many times. I love good stories, especially when they're personal. I believe they grow better with each telling.

Stories are situational. Heraclitus warned, "You could not step twice into the same rivers, for other waters are ever flowing on to you...." I am different each time I listen, and emphasize new and subtle aspects each time I tell. I live, work, reflect, learn, adapt, and move forward. We always have choices.

As a young man, I thought Frost's poem focused on decisions

and actions. Now I see the unconscious, and sometimes deliberate, steps I took, seldom understanding all the risks, benefits, and consequences.

The essays are intended to stimulate conversations.

I've read the stories in this volume many times. I know each author well, and each has surprised me, more than once. I recruited the writers but did not assign topics, preferring instead to foster creativity, hear their personal work stories, and encourage them to discover and strengthen their own voices. WDI will host regional forums, where authors will present their stories and listeners will be invited to share theirs. We all learn through dialogue and strengthen our communities when we find common ground. When one of us speaks distinctly with an authentic voice, this helps others understand their own experiences.

Everyone in this book is a reflective practitioner: from labor leaders to executives, from program administrators to activists and observers. We are all storytellers. Like Kahlil Gibran, we act as if "work is love made visible." These stories reflect our lives, work, commitments, what we have learned, and how we developed our skills, insights and aspirations.

We wrote to learn, to share a few lessons, and to focus our priorities; to understand ourselves and to celebrate what we know.

To express oneself is to be human. Each of us believes in the dignity of work. We know that labor and working families must have strong voices to speak up for those who feel unseen and/or undervalued. We are not the only ones who can write, but since we can, we do. We have clarified our understanding of work while writing, and expect to learn more through dialogue.

This project emerged after I was honored by Rockefeller College of Public Affairs & Policy, University at Albany (SUNY), receiving their Distinguished Continuing Professional Education Leadership Award of Excellence. What pleased me most was when Professor Eugene J. Monaco described me as a "reflective practitioner," an example of what Donald Schön wrote about in his book by that same name. I felt valued and seen. This is something we all need.

With pride and humility, I am a reflective practitioner. I am not the only one. I am surrounded by equally deserving colleagues who are motivated by clear values, know where they come from, advocate for working families, and mentor and guide younger workers. In accepting the award, I felt a responsibility to pay it forward and invite those whom I respect to share their insights and publish their personal stories in order to foster a broader conversation.

Growing up, most of us were warned not to brag. We were trained to write objectively; to let the facts speak for our opinions, rather than put ourselves into the story. I am more interested in people than theory. I chose to be an implementer, knowing that progress does not happen on its own. We need leaders. I learn more from intelligent and reflective activists and subjective, personal, and practical narratives. Each author was asked to write a personal narrative. Each is a leader, an innovator, and a storyteller. They tell us what they know of life, and that's how we all learn.

Leaders need to understand themselves to serve their constituency, to know their assets, be aware of their deficits, and recognize when and how personal distortions can damage an organization. We have seen great leaders who used their experience and strengths to accomplish wonders, and others who let personal demons sabotage their dreams.

As the founder and Executive Director of the Workforce Development Institute (WDI), I helped develop a non-profit partnership with the New York State AFL-CIO, committed to serving working families and strengthening society through workforce, economic, and community development. WDI is a strong and effective organization. We have statewide and regional operations, strategic partnerships that enable us to add value in many situations. I take great pride in our capacity, services, manufacturing and economic development grants, technical assistance, education and training programs, child care subsidies, environmental and cultural services, and advocacy for those who have been marginalized. WDI is a leader-full organization in partnership with and supported by a network of advocates, from unions to government, businesses, and communities.

# WORKING STORIES

In this collection I outline my path to leadership, and others share theirs too. You won't find blueprints. You'll discover guideposts to navigate calm and rough waters while we all invented who we became. I hope this book will foster an inter-generational dialogue. Each writer's story inspired me to understand WDI's mission better, made my commitment to serve workers stronger, and broadened my perspective. Be prepared to be inspired.

It is story time. "Once upon a time, there was a reflective practitioner...."

# WHY THE MIDDLE IS THE ANSWER

Vivian Benton

Years ago, I had two friends who had an argument. If you talked to the first one, you came away thinking that the other one was completely wrong. If you talked to the second one, you came away believing that the first one was all wrong. It was really difficult to try to help resolve the differences, until I began to understand that the truth was somewhere in the middle. Both parties were so entrenched in the belief that they were right that both of them were putting forward some truths, some untruths or half-truths, exaggerations, etc. Once I accepted that fact, it was easier to work around it.

Politics today is much the same way. The left despises the right. The right despises the left. There is not a lot of collaboration or work toward the common good. The bumper stickers I see all over New York State about repealing the Secure Ammunition and Firearms Enforcement (SAFE) Act is a good example. There is no middle ground on this issue for some people.

How do we work around this when the issues are even larger, such as workforce development, jobs, and economic development across all of New York State? How do we not get mired in the arguments, bureaucracy, and political stands, and make some progress?

I work for a small non-profit—the Workforce Development Institute (WDI)—that tries very hard to stay in the middle and do just that. It's difficult in New York State, but not impossible. This particular non-profit is aligned with organized labor. While much of what we do is influenced by our alignment with labor, the bulk of our work is non-union-related and spans a wide range of projects, all focused on filling gaps in the current New York State workforce development system, and then moving programs that work well across the state. Our goals and policies have been established with a "middle-of-the-road" feel, or, just enough procedures to ensure good management, but enough wiggle room to be able to provide assistance on a wide variety of workforce-related issues.

When I started at this non-profit, I was new to the New York State system and to the small non-profit system that is beholden to state and federal grants and contracts for survival. I was amazed, and often frustrated, by the obstacles we faced simply to do business. Bureaucracy and a lack of coordination among agencies seemed to be around every corner. The bureaucratic "this is the way we've always done things" way of thinking can be found everywhere, not just in government agencies. I believe strongly in the union movement when it works well, but we do see unions losing membership, in part, due to that "no change" mentality. The work environment today has changed since the days when unions first took hold in New York State, and the union movement needs to change with it.

I've learned—largely through the people I've worked with over the years—how to make things work and use some advantages of the small non-profit to stand out and help move the bar a little higher for all. Along the way, my own views on politics and collaboration have shifted. I feel more strongly that the moderate middle is the place where progress happens, and that we all need to step back and look at the bigger picture more often.

### My Harvard Background–A Learning Experience

My experience at the WDI has been an eye-opener. I came to New York State after 15 years at Harvard Medical School (HMS), where I started as a junior financial analyst and ended as the Director of Financial Operations and Analysis.

I have always considered myself very fortunate, for a few reasons, to have landed my first job at HMS. First, the HMS environment was much more complicated—both programmatically and financially—than what I had anticipated. HMS was not just a medical school, but had various lines of business that all required very different types of planning and management, so I was exposed to a wide variety of business and planning problems. Second, and probably more importantly, I found myself working in a "matrix" environment, reporting to any number of administrative leaders—the Director of Financial Analysis, the Dean for Finance, the Dean for Planning, the Dean for Facilities and Operations— depending on the project. All of these administrators were hired by, and reported to, the Executive Dean for Management and Administration, who was a force to be reckoned with. This particular dean was very smart, and loved to play the role of devil's advocate on virtually every topic. His goal was to ensure that all possible avenues had been thought through and vetted thoroughly before a final proposal was put forth. This dean set a tone for excellence that trickled down to all levels of administration and forced us to think critically about everything we did. No one wanted to be caught unprepared or be unable to answer questions in front of him. The result was that HMS was light-years ahead of the other Harvard schools (or any school, I would argue) in terms of management and administration. I worked extremely hard during these years—late nights and most weekends—but was happy to do so, as I always felt that I had been given opportunities right from the start that I would not have received elsewhere. I learned a tremendous amount during these years on a variety of topics— critical thinking, writing, presenting, understanding which facts matter and when, prioritizing, collaborating, etc. Although the job was in the Finance Department, my job went far beyond the financial realm. I never thought only about the finances. Rather, I learned the importance of the program first, how the financial plan could support it, and how a change in one area of the school could have ripple effects elsewhere. I learned how this large, complicated puzzle that was Harvard Medical School fit together. I became a "resident expert" on all things related to finance and planning. It was a hard job—extremely demanding for 15 years—but also very rewarding, and I truly liked the environment and the people with whom I worked.

Compared to my work at WDI later on, HMS was quite different in a number of ways. For one thing, there were significant resources at HMS. During my 15 years there, I worked under two different, but progressive, deans. When the dean had an idea and wanted to move on something, we had the resources and the administrative team to do it and to do it well. Occasionally, there were some issues that took longer to address, but, for the most part, if the dean or his advisers wanted something to happen, it did. New curricula were developed. Buildings were built. Departments were merged and new departments created. Faculty was recruited from around the world and initiatives were launched. When I look back at all the significant changes that occurred at HMS during my 15 years there, I feel very fortunate to have had the opportunity to be a part of it. Again, we had the resources, the initiative, and the know-how. And the administrative team was just that—a team. We were successful in moving projects forward.

While even Harvard Medical School had financial problems that had to be managed, overall, I was relatively insulated from issues such as cash flow (the University managed the cash for all its Schools) and government contracts taking months to be finalized (the university simply bore the risk and responsibility until the contracts were finalized and cash came through).

During my years in Boston, I considered myself very much on the political left. I am the daughter of a liberal arts professor. I lived and worked in a very liberal city for 15 years. I did not understand the issues raised by the right regarding government bureaucracy or the "business first" attitude at all.

I left HMS by choice after I had twins later in life. When my twins turned three, I realized I wanted to move back to New York State to be closer to family, and that perhaps the demanding job I had held for years was too much to manage while raising twin toddlers. I left Boston without a job lined up in New York State, but with the idea that I would perhaps work at something not as demanding. I distinctly remember my boss telling me that I would never find another work environment like the one I was leaving. I agreed with her but was not worried about it, since it was a slower pace of life that I was after.

### An Eye-Opener-WDI

I found my job at WDI by answering a blind newspaper ad. The ad noted that an unnamed non-profit was looking for a finance director to manage a growing budget. That was all I knew about the position. When I was interviewed, I remember being concerned that I might be bored here, after having managed a very complicated $300 million budget. By contrast, the WDI budget was small, and seemed relatively straightforward. However, I also remember the executive director telling me that he had narrowed the final candidates to two individuals. The first was a "meat and potatoes" finance profession-al, who would see to it that everything was taken care of in terms of finance, but likely would not expand beyond a strictly financial role. The second was me. He explained very clearly that he wanted to grow the organization in different ways and define a role for WDI within New York State, and for that, he needed someone who would help him plan and grow the company, operating outside of a financial role. If I was interested in this role, then I would be his candidate. I accepted the role. And, while I had worried about being bored, what I found was a host of new and different challenges and learning expe-riences that I had never encountered at HMS.

My initial year at WDI was quite an eye-opener, particularly in terms of understanding the bureaucracy involved in getting money to show up on time. Putting projects on hold and waiting for contracts to wend their way through the state system became the norm. Cash took forever to come through. Vendors were asked to wait, and they complained. We looked bad as a business because we could not pay those we owed on time and almost missed making our own payroll more than once. I remember venting to my boss about the State taking forever to pay what they owed, and I remember being floored when he commented that "we would not be the first non-profit that went under waiting for the State to pay."

Add to this the learning experience I had around the New York State workforce and economic development systems themselves. It seemed that we were constantly learning of inequities, negative incentives, and the ineffectiveness of large and unconnected bureaucracies. I remember asking, naively, why economic development was separate from workforce development. Other questions followed. Why were there no repercussions when a company received 10 years of tax breaks, then promptly moved at the 10-year mark? Why was there no understanding of implications (loss of income taxes, loss of local spending, increases to unemployment) around the use of local versus out-of-state labor for building projects? Why were there so many rules and regulations around grants available for businesses that it was virtually impossible for any small- or medium-sized business to apply? Why did some of the community colleges and Workforce Investment Boards seem so far removed from the employers whom they were supposed to be serving?

And then there were issues around support for the workers. At Harvard, our Human Resources Department tracked very carefully when a department started to bump up against the six-month mark when using temporary services. I remember well the mantra of the HR director: "If someone starts looking and smelling like an employee, it's time to convert them and give them benefits." So, then, why did we see so many companies making use of long-term temporary services, denying higher pay and benefits to individuals who "looked and smelled" like employees?

At first I thought that maybe I wasn't fully understanding the issues. Now I know that I was understanding the issues, and that my Harvard experience had, in fact, trained me to ask all the right questions. The answer, however, was that nothing was happening to address the issues. Also, I began to understand that the answers, just like in my HMS experience, were not always black and white. Just because something may not make perfect sense financially, it may still make sense to move forward on it if the programmatic implications could have significant pay-off down the road. I began to see that perhaps changes around the edges could help lead to larger changes. I also began to understand how a small non-profit such as the WDI can help facilitate some of these changes. However, sometimes there need to be some compromises around how to do that.

## How to Make a Difference? Resourceful Policies and Recognition That the Answers Are Not Black or White

My experience at WDI has shifted my thinking on a number of issues. Primarily, I've come to understand that it's not all about business and it's not all about the worker; it's a combination. Policy should not be focused on one or the other, but on both at the same time. The end result will likely be some sort of middle-ground—not ideal to either side, but a compromise.

I think a common mistake on the part of government, large corporations, and unions is that they don't pay enough attention to what is occurring on the ground. Information is collected, but is often interpreted incorrectly. Too much attention is paid to formulating incredibly restrictive guidelines, so that responses are so inflexible they're not helpful, and sometimes even backfire. Often, responses target one particular group without a lot of thought about the impact to others.

So how has WDI, a small non-profit, made a difference in a system that seems polarized and rigid? The answers include a curious staff who are encouraged to think outside the box, ground-level (street) information, a flexibility of resources, responsiveness and a lack of complexity, and the ability to make connections. I give my boss credit for repeatedly hammering these points home. The result is that, for a small agency, we make a large impact.

### Curious and Open-minded Staff

WDI's executive director has always maintained that hiring good staff is paramount. We're a small entity, so one bad recruit can hamper what we do. As such, we take recruiting seriously, and the screening process for new staff is probably the only area where we have a tendency to go through a laborious process. Staff must be curious (with a capital "C") about how things work, and how programs and resources might fit together. One of WDI's strengths is that we've recruited curious extroverts, who make it their business to scan news articles, attend meetings, talk to a variety of individuals, and then "pound the pavement" within their regions to gather more information about company plans and workforce issues. The staff is good at collecting information about what is happening in their respective regions that might impact workforce development. It's interesting to note that several of our regional staff members have extensive union backgrounds that initially scared some companies off. In fact, we hired them precisely because they spoke about what they liked and did not like about what they had seen within the union movement, and how they would change things if they could. That ability to be open to new ideas and to want to be helpful is key.

### Ground-Level Information

It seems that a lot of state policy requires data, data, and more data. Our perspective on what is happening in a given region comes more from a "boots on the ground" orientation. Data is good, but it needs to be backed up by being out in the field and collecting information anecdotally as well; from employers, non-profits, unions, and others. The ground-level information can either back up or dispel what data might indicate is a "trend". This, too, I view as a middle-of-the-road approach. One source or the other should not be the be-all and end-all.

### Flexibility of Resources

The dollars given to WDI are relatively flexible. In addition, our mission is broad. We are interested in programs that have a positive impact on jobs. This could be job growth, job retention, or job promotion (moving individuals up the career ladder). As a result, we are not hemmed in by the rigidity of many government grant programs. For example, many government programs that deal with job growth are focused only on putting the long-term unemployed to work.

However, jump-starting job growth can happen in many ways. We've had small manufacturers ask for help with equipment or software. Sometimes a relatively small change in the way they do business can help them go after and win additional contracts, and then quickly grow their staff. We've had other companies ask for help with incumbent worker training in order to help move individuals up the career ladder. The baby boomer generation is getting ready to retire and incumbent worker training—or getting individuals ready to take the place of those retiring—is a significant need. By helping a company promote current employees, new positions open up at the junior level, and the result is new job placements. What we've found is that flexibility needs to be built into policy, rather than extreme positions around serving specific groups.

### Responsiveness and Lack of Complexity

The WDI has instituted systems, policies, and procedures for a company, union, non-profit, or other entity to apply for help, and also to report back on the outcome of the program. Our system is purposely not overly complicated. Feedback from the field is that the small- or medium-sized company, non-profit, or other entity does not have the resources to devote to a cumbersome grant process. Our goal is to help move programming and have a positive impact on jobs as quickly as possible, and so our systems are designed to accomplish just that. Again, the idea that policies and procedures are necessary, but should be instituted in a way that does not impede action, is more of a "middle-of-the-road" approach. Also, the ability to look at those policies and procedures and adapt them to changes in the field is important. We try hard to do both.

### Ability to Connect the Dots

The WDI staff is instructed to be on the lookout for programs that lead to good jobs, not just any jobs. We have a fiduciary responsibility not to invest in programs where individuals are not likely to be successful, or where a company does not treat its workers well. For example, if a company has a very high turnover rate, we want to understand why before we devote resources to helping it. Is it the wage? Is it the working conditions? Will we sink dollars into a training program, only to have the staff that has been recruited leave almost immediately?

WDI is not a provider of services, but, rather, a connector, a facilitator, a collaborator, and a funder. Because our staff makes it their business to understand their regions, they are good at identifying trends, connecting companies to resources, and determining what programs will have a positive impact on good jobs. We have no ulterior motives, other than to help grow good jobs in New York State.

### Bottom Line

The bottom line in all of this is that we try very hard to understand both sides of the story. The business needs to make a profit, but the worker needs to earn a living wage. There has been a lot in the national media about the loss of middle-class America and the growth of the very wealthy and the working-poor classes. The return of jobs that pay better—manufacturing and certain service-sector jobs—is a real possibility if we use our resources and direct policy wisely. We are at a crossroads here. Businesses need help, but they should not get it at the expense of the working individual. WDI makes a difference by investing in programs and directing programs that have a positive impact on both the company and the individual. The understanding that there are two sides to every story is incredibly important to what we do, and why we have been successful.

As for my own personal journey, it's interesting that the two organizations at which I've spent the bulk of my career are so different in terms of mission and wealth, but alike in other ways. Both pushed staff to think differently, to reflect on what you're doing before doing it, and to remember to "see the forest through the trees." The result—at least in terms of shaping my own thinking—is that it often moves me to a middle ground on fiscal and program issues.

I remember interviewing a candidate for a WDI regional director position, who noted during the interview that, "If someone has a very different opinion from me, I try to take a step back and ask some questions about it. I try to put myself in that person's shoes. I try to understand how that person views the problem, and why." He got the job.

# WORKING STORIES

# WHO I AM

Jim Bertolone

## Who I Am

A baby boomer born in 1951 and now a "geezer boomer," or
close to it. We lived with my paternal grandparents in my early years
in Rochester, New York. My great-grandparents came here from Sic-
ily when my grandparents were between the ages of 8 and 10 years
old, between 1908-1912. Even after we got our own place to live,
I spent much time staying at my grandparents' home. My parents'
generation, which grew up during the Great Depression, worked
multiple jobs into the 1960s. My mother also worked, between
having four children, just like many growing up today as working
poor. In the 1950s, TV shows like *Leave it to Beaver* and *Father
Knows Best* were so far removed from our experience, they might
as well have been filmed on Mars. My mother was from a family of
15 children; my father, the youngest of four. The Sicilian-American
neighborhood we lived in was known as "Mount Allegro," which
would become the title of a book about that neighborhood, written by
a neighbor, Jerre Mangione. Mr. Mangione wrote that book as part
of Franklin D. Roosevelt's Federal Writers' Project, part of the New
Deal's Keynesian efforts to sustain the arts community during the
Great Depression. When I was a young man, my father would get me
an autographed copy of that book when Jerre Mangione came to visit
Rochester. By this time, he was Professor Mangione, of the Universi-

ty of Pennsylvania. Jerre Mangione's brother lived around the corner and had a small grocery store, and loved jazz. Somehow, Mr. Mangione talked one of the greats on the jazz circuit, one Dizzy Gillespie, to give his son Chuck trumpet lessons. The Mangione boys were seven to nine years older than I was, but Chuck and Gap Mangione would do all right in the music world.

### 1960-1961 ... The Awakening Begins

My father was a voracious reader, as I was fast becoming with the help of the tax-supported bookmobile. This was kind of a bus library, bringing books to lend to city neighborhoods. In 1963, at the age of 12, I began the habit of reading the morning paper every day, as I had to deliver it to pay a debt from an early brush with the law. Thus, I got the paper at least an hour before everyone else, and enjoyed getting the news and baseball box scores first. However, the awakening to real history and political machinations began at age 9, in 1960, when I watched the Kennedy-Nixon debates with my father. My father was a strong Kennedy supporter, but it probably didn't matter who the Democratic nominee was, because he disliked Nixon with a passion. During the debates, I got filled in on the Hughes Loan, the Checkers speech, Nixon's connections to the House Un-American Activities Committee (HUAC), Senator McCarthy, red-baiting, and the blacklisting and destruction of one of my father's favorite actors, John Garfield. Needless to say, my father, a union man, did not think too much of the president of the actors' union who was helping to blacklist his own union members. The SAG president was a "B" actor, Ronald Reagan. White reactionary backlash to the Civil Rights Movement, the anti-war movement, inner-city riots, and culture shock would lead to Nixon's comeback and the rise of Ronald Reagan. Interestingly, it seemed to me that too many of the conservative "law and order" crowd did not seem to have a problem with terrorism and murder, as long as it was visited on people of color, civil rights advocates, or anti-war demonstrators.

## The Move And Civil Rights

In the summer of 1961, my parents bought a house off Lyell Avenue, still a working-class neighborhood with many Italian-Americans, but not exclusively, like the Sicilian-American community of "Mount Allegro." It was a step up. It would take less than a month and we would be outcasts to most of the neighbors. The school year that began in the fall of 1961 would also be the first year of busing in order to achieve school integration. It was strictly voluntary, and we were not being forced to go to school out of our neighborhood. However, more than 30 African-American kids would be bused to our school. Many of the neighbors were up in arms and organized a boycott; they would keep their kids home from school in protest. I was entering fifth grade, the oldest of four, with my brother Vinnie entering third grade. Much of what I was hearing was uncomfortable, but also above my head. My father sat down with my brother and me, and told us we would go to school. He said that the reason his parents and my mother's parents came to this country was for a fair shot. He said that it was not about equality; that no two people in the whole world were exactly equal. He said that the promise of this country was equal opportunity and equality of treatment under the law. That if you were honest and willing to work, you had the same opportunity as anyone else to make something of your life. "Those kids have as much right to go to that school as you, and you will go to school." Not all, but most, kept their kids home from school for nearly two weeks. A few years later, and in retrospect, I would be very proud of my father that day. However, at the time, and already having some issues with both anger and authority, I was more thrilled that I had my father's permission to defy the other adults in the neighborhood. How cool was that! I went to school those first two weeks, a new school for us, walking the few blocks with a defiant smile all the way. By weeks three and four, the boycott began to fade, though there were a few kids sent to Catholic schools who never came back.

## Race Becomes Personal

When I was in school, high school was ninth grade through twelfth grade. Once puberty came, my olive skin would become very dark in the summer from living on the playground and always playing ball. My curly hair became tight and kinky, like two of my cousins'. My cousin Mike and I were sometimes referred to as "Spook and Spic," and one of the mildest nicknames in high school was "Brillo." Into this mix, the '60s were unfolding, and I was becoming more and more aware of civil rights issues and confrontations and the rejections of establishment thinking. At home, ethnic slurs were not tolerated by my father, and at school, a high school history teacher made me question and think critically. What I was hearing and seeing from too many people on issues of race would cause me some serious issues with authority. I could not respect any adult who used the N word. Though I had always been on the Honor Roll in grammar school, and had made Standard Bearer, supposedly the honor that went to the male with the highest scholastic achievement, high school was different. I got thrown out of school five times, every year from eighth grade to senior year. As luck would have it, I always scored well on Regents finals and did well on the SAT and Regents Scholarship Test. This, along with playing four years of high school football and baseball and voted by peers and coaches as an All City/All Scholastic outfielder, my senior year seemed to cancel out my discipline issues, as I applied to five colleges and was accepted by all of them, Notre Dame included. Economics would dictate a state college, where, with a partial Regents scholarship, I could work my way through with $200-a-semester tuition. The propaganda of the free market apologists has denied such a similar opportunity to today's young people.

## My Father as Dr. Frankenstein

When I left home to go to State college in 1969, there were three younger siblings at home.

My freshman year in college, 1969-1970, I think my father began to worry that teaching me to stand up for what I believed in was going to cause me a hard life, including the possibility of jail. There were civil rights and anti-war picket lines, and a takeover of a college building and student strike after Kent State and Jackson State in May of 1970. Having African-American friends brought, along with my own natural Afro, more police stops and police scrutiny. The divisions of the '60s have been covered *ad nauseam*, WWII generation versus anti-Vietnam, white versus black, integration versus bootstraps, and "a man's home is his castle," second-class status versus women's rights, etc. My father, a World War II veteran, knew guys whom I knew, and their families, where Vietnam hit close to home, sometimes painfully so. He educated himself on Vietnam and other issues. I had a student deferment entering state college in September 1969, for about 30 days. Nixon classified us all 1-A for the first draft lottery in December 1969. This would turn out to be a lottery that I would win, with number 275. These and other dynamics had my father, unlike many of his peers, moving more to the left, not the right.

### Nixon And The Strike

Our old nemesis, Nixon, was back, and was now the president. I think many moderates and liberals were aghast at the anti-war movement in the mid-to-late1960s, because they voted for President Johnson and felt he was sincere. This was the man who passed Kennedy's Civil Rights Act, said "We shall overcome" on TV to pass the Voting Rights Act, stood up to the Klan, and tried to conquer poverty. However, after Nixon got elected, many of these people already knew Nixon as mean-spirited, manipulative, and untrustworthy, and older generations began to question the reasons we were in Vietnam. Economic issues, always there, got tougher for a lot of people, and particularly for postal workers, like my father and his brothers. Nixon's promises to postal workers were worthless. Underpaid for years, a promised raise was undercut, and real injustice was felt by postal workers.

### Uncle Sam v. Postal Workers

My father and three uncles were in the Postal Unions.

# WORKING STORIES

On St. Patrick's Day in 1970, postal workers had had enough, and wildcat strikes began in New York City, and spread. Before the computer age, stocks, payrolls, bank transactions, trade at New York City ports, and most all business was done through the mail. Commerce and profits took a large hit. Nixon called out the Army and National Guard. They could not deliver the mail and, unlike Kent State and Jackson State less than two months later, there were no bullets or violence visited on the strikers. Top pay for a postal clerk or letter carrier in 1970 was about $8,400 per year after 21 years of service, about 25% below the poverty-level threshold for a family of four in New York State. About 20% of postal workers in New York City were eligible for food stamps. In 1969, my freshman year in college, I qualified for a National Defense Student Loan, and you had to be under the poverty level to qualify. Needless to say, winning that illegal strike and gaining the right to collectively bargain on wages and benefits would bring postal workers solidly into the middle class.

When I left home to go to state college in 1969, there were three younger siblings at home. Because we were under the poverty-level, there was no money for school. At that time, environmental issues came to the fore: Love Canal, an occasional river catching on fire, and the closing of Lake Ontario, as well as some of the other Great Lakes, to swimmers. The fish were not edible and swimmers were becoming ill from the pollution. I got a seasonal job digging holes for and constructing all types of swimming pools, from concrete in the ground to redwood and other above-ground pools. For the next four summers, we could barely keep up with the demand, and I made good money for those days.

As 1973 approached, I had the maximum hours allowed, at that time, in my History major and a Political Science minor, and had completed the Liberal Arts core, and was being scheduled to student teach. I decided that teaching was not my calling, and I got tired of being broke, so I left school.

Not long after I left college, the 1973 recession hit, driven by OPEC, where gas doubled from about 36 cents a gallon to over 70 cents. Rochester's Big Three, Kodak, Bausch & Lomb, and Xerox, were not hiring, and the two large auto plants were laying off. Jobs were tough.

I would spend six months grinding steel as a tool & die apprentice, with a base six-day, 49-hour schedule.

I had taken some Civil Service tests, and when the Postal Service called in September 1973, I decided to try that. Of course, with my family's general union background and, specifically, postal unions (father and three uncles), I joined the American Postal Workers Union the same day. My first "legal" job, with work papers, at age 16 in 1967-68, was also a union job, in a large grocery chain represented at that time by the Retail Clerks International Union.

It has often been said that bad bosses are often union's best organizers, and the Postal Service was no different. New employees, especially "Subs," were talked down to and treated poorly, and I was not having any of it. I went to union meetings from the start, served on an Election Committee, and was a union steward for the afternoon shift by 1974. All positions were elected, and in 1978, I became the Clerk Craft Director, the largest of the four crafts that made up my union. By 1983, I was a full-time advocate and had completed the Labor Studies program at the Cornell School of Industrial and Labor Relations, and spent many years on their State Board. By 1990, I was the president of my Local. My predecessor, Larry Tuchrello, mentored me and believed in me. So did National President Moe Biller, out of New York City's Lower East Side and the leader in 1970, along with Vince Sombrotto of the Letter Carriers, of the wildcat strike that gave postal workers collective bargaining and NLRB rights.

Moe Biller would appoint me to the first group of National Arbitration Advocates in the early 1980s, and I was assigned cases in New York, Philadelphia, Chicago, and at headquarters in Washington, D.C. Moe was a friend who trusted me because I never asked him for anything, and had turned down National Union positions elected and appointed, including in the top half-dozen spots as, by this time, I would not relocate to Washington, D.C., NYC, or Philly.

In addition to family and some mentors who believed in me, it was always the union members. First the WWII generation, like my father, who believed in me and said "you're our guy and the future." The Postal Service is the largest civilian employer of veterans due to veteran preference in hiring. I was honored to be their advocate as Korea's vets and Vietnam vets were also entering the Postal Service. We are also the largest civilian employer of African-Americans, minorities, and women. I remain honored to represent those historically denied a fair shake.

### AFL-CIO

I was recruited to the executive board of my CLC by Chris Garlock, who would leave in a couple of years to produce Jim Hightower's radio show in Austin, Texas. He is now the lead staff in Washington, D.C.'s, Labor Federation. We moved the CLC to put the leaders of two dozen unions on the executive board in order to build power. I was asked to deliver the keynote speech at Workers' Memorial Day in 1995, after the Oklahoma domestic terrorist bombing that killed so many, including children in daycare. It was possibly my most passionate and angry speech, and attacked our own fascists, from the KKK, Nazi Skinheads, and G. Gordon Liddy, who had advocated shooting at federal employees' heads because they wear bulletproof vests. The speech must have moved a few as, even though it was only a few minutes long, it appeared word-for-word on TV and in the newspaper. By the end of 1997, I was the consensus new president of the CLC.

In 2001, Moe Biller appointed me as his designee for the New Alliance, which would result in Area Labor Federation. I have gotten to know and work with so many great people from labor, WDI, and non-profits, and have met with Congress and senators, and Cesar Chavez, Jesse Jackson, Bill Lucy, and others from CBTU.

### Civil Rights, Labor Rights, And Conservatives

When I was 17, like many, I had an epiphany when Martin Luther King, Jr. was murdered while standing with black sanitation workers in Memphis. Workers demanding the right to unionize and bargain for living wages and safe working conditions. Meeting Cesar Chavez and supporting the rights of farm workers led many of us to believe that civil rights and workers' rights were part of the same struggle, the struggle for human rights. My studies as a History major, and life experience, would lead me to the conclusion that one cannot be conservative in our society and be a union advocate. It is a contradiction. Conservatives opposed every bit of progress toward equal rights and justice for all. Conservatives opposed American independence and supported the English Crown, the Tories. The Conservative Right opposed all progress toward justice in our history. They supported slavery and child labor. They were against equal rights and integration. They stood against equal rights for women, the Voting Rights Act, the Civil Rights Act. They stood against workers' rights, collective bargaining, a minimum wage, the eight-hour workday, public education, Medicare, and Social Security.

Most of these things were the platform of Democratic Socialists, like Norman Thomas and, later, Martin Luther King, Jr. both strong anti-communists, a distinction lost on most Americans. Progressives on the left would move these items forward, and many would begin to become law during the New Deal and/or the 1960s. With the rise of Milton Friedman, and the free market the answer to all problems, leading to Reagan, the pendulum has swung to the right. Equal rights, economic justice, and political justice have regressed. As unions have been targeted and weakened, we now have 42% of Americans working for less than $15 per hour, and wealth inequality has returned to the days of the Robber Barons and the Gilded Age. The English writer and philosopher, John Stewart Mill said, before the middle of the 19th century after touring America, that "not all conservatives are stupid, but all stupid people are conservatives." The only reason to form a democracy is so that the people can protect themselves from the rich and powerful. The problem with believing in small, limited central government is that power abhors a vacuum. What we see today are the rich and powerful, individuals, corporations, and banksters filling that power vacuum at the expense of a people's democracy.

If you tell me you are conservative but a union advocate, you are telling me you are confused and/or ignorant.

We must strive to be open-minded, while thinking critically; strive to know history; and always follow the money. We can move the arc back toward justice, and we must.

As for my own life, I've had a rich and satisfying union career. I ran for office in my own Local for 42 years. I had opposition once, and 80% of my members cast a secret ballot to elect me by 7 to 1. Since 1998, I have been president of the CLC, and since 2002, of the Area Labor Federation, unopposed each time. I am grateful to all these workers who have supported me, and I owe a debt I cannot repay. I am committed to doing what I am most passionate about, do what I most believe in for my life's work, and make a living at it. I thank and owe them all.

# WE NEED ROSES ALONGSIDE OUR BREAD

## Esther Cohen

*Hearts Starve, As Well As Bodies;*
*Give Us Bread, But Give Us Roses, Too.*
—"Bread and Roses," James Oppenheim
Lawrence, Massachusetts (1912)

Every story has many beginnings.

One of mine starts in Ansonia, Connecticut, the factory town of 20,000 people where I grew up, a place of heavy machine manufacturing. The town's nickname is The Copper City. I spent 18 years in this factory town, home of Farrel-Birmingham ball bearings, an old union town, where fair pay and fair work were what we knew was right. Working is in the DNA of the town itself.

Many paths are circuitous and unpredictable. My grandparents on both sides were Eastern European immigrants. They left their homes for the reasons most people do: life became impossible in the countries where they lived. My mother's family went from Romania to Grand Forks, North Dakota. My father's father traveled from Vilna, Lithuania, to Johannesburg, South Africa, and then to Ansonia, Connecticut. Reasons why things happen always come after. My grandfather was a learned man. In Ansonia, he was a merchant in a factory town. He sold men's suits and family shoes, and wrote letters in English for anyone who needed them, at an oak desk in the back of the store, called Oscar Cohen's. Factories and workers were part of our lives. What we see and how we see it has been one of my lifelong obsessions. Maybe one reason is that what my ancestors saw outside their windows in different times and different places was so different from what was outside my own window as a child.

In Ansonia, I saw big brick factories, and the Housatonic River running right through town, and a crooked Main Street connecting us all.

Because stories are not linear—not really— my life floated by. I wanted to be a writer, and I thought, in the misguided way of the young, that writing would be easier in New York City, the city I've now lived in for most of my life. Books were my theology, my belief system. It was the '70s, and the world was turbulent, and vocal. Demonstrating for what you felt was a part of every day. The world was a mess, and the response of so many of us was to protest: to join together and stand in the streets. To figure out ways of making the world better, even a little.

I held many jobs. I've never been on a track of any kind. I'd work for a while, and then travel, going to live in another country, to see what life might look like there. And I rationalized all my jobs, saying that they were part of the stories I would tell. Every single thing has the potential to be a Good Story. That was good enough for me.

Years went by, the way they do.

Through a college friend, a man named Stephen whom I had met at a party because he had memorized the entire book of Thomas Wolfe's *Look Homeward Angel* (a feat I admire to this day), I met Dr. Paul Sherry. He was a wise theologian, a disciple of Reinhold Niebuhr, a Protestant ethicist who wrote serious and significant books about public affairs and social policy. Paul was born in the hard coal regions of Pennsylvania, in a town of miners and their families. He loved the town, and his life was shaped by the people he met as a boy; people he was determined to help as much as he could. He studied union organizing with Saul Alinsky, but Alinsky and other union people felt he'd be happier as a man of the church, and he ended up going to Union Seminary.

Paul became a Protestant minister and, later, the publisher of The Pilgrim Press, an illustrious old American publishing house. They say it was the first.

He hired me to publish books on social justice. My job interview question: Is justice a theological or philosophical idea? I said: Both.

I've worked on books since high school; putting them together, fixing sentences, ordering chapters. My mandate at Pilgrim was to acquire books that were about social issues: death row, labor, income inequality, homelessness. Paul was a high-minded man, someone who worked in a variety of ways to make life better. He talked a lot about justice, and injustice, and what we could all do. He hoped that books could change people's minds, could affect the social dialogue. He believed in books the way I did.

Although I've never been without a book alongside my bed, they were always novels, stories, poems. At Pilgrim Press, I started thinking about books as advocacy tools; books as stories that could change the way the reader thought.

We would have lunch with potential authors every day. Many were academics or theologians of various kinds, and they were often ponderous, often dull, but one day, Paul brought a labor leader into my office, a man named Moe Foner. Moe came from a family that helped shape the left wing of the labor movement, the famous Foner brothers. When we met, in the '80s, he was running Bread and Roses, the non-profit cultural arm of 1199, a union with a long history on the left, including working with Dr. King during the Sanitation Workers' Strike and protesting against the war in Vietnam. It was a union of low-wage hospital workers and homecare workers, largely women of color, who joined picket lines and marches as part of their work.

Moe was a tall, funny, extremely persuasive talker. He could sell anything to his listener, and often did. At lunch, he would share many ideas he had for books, but two in particular struck a chord. He wanted to reissue a book about the Bread and Roses strike, in Lawrence, Massachusetts, in 1912, where women and children fought for child labor laws. The book had been written by his friend, William Cahan. For the cover, we would use a beautiful Ralph Fasanella painting. Fasanella was an artist from the Electrical Workers Union. Moe helped send him to Lawrence, Massachusetts, to paint the town where the strike had taken place.

The Cahan book was full of photographs taken by Lewis Hine: schoolchildren working in the textile mill and pictures of the town of Lawrence. The story of Lawrence, Massachusetts, was a large, important American story that many were unfamiliar with. It was a story about how women and children banded together, with the help of the Wobblies, and how they changed the child labor laws, and the history of American labor.

Maybe it was how Moe told the story, or how ignorant I was of labor history, but the combination of culture and narrative in working history seemed, very suddenly, like what I wanted to do. Even more: what I had to do.

His second idea was to create an exhibit, at the Bread and Roses Gallery at 1199's headquarters. 1199 was the only labor union with a full-time gallery. It was a small space in the lobby of the union's headquarters at 310 West 43rd Street. As part of his notion of providing both Bread and Roses, Moe felt it was important for union members and staff to have the opportunity to see art of all kinds on a regular basis.

He wanted to create an exhibit with quotations from labor history, called Images of Labor, assigning the quotations to a wide range of artists, to creatively depict what it meant to be a worker. Working, in our society in particular, is such a complicated notion. Many people don't want to be thought of as workers, although, of course, we all are. They want to be understood in other ways—as professionals, maybe; implying that the work that professionals do is not exactly work but, rather, a higher vocation.

How is it that some ideas become intrinsic parts of our lives? My guess is that—like so much of life—mystery, chance, and fortune all play a role. And for me, language does too.

Bread and Roses seemed to belong together in an important way, a way that I too wanted to tell people. The work Moe did was the work I wanted to do: combining culture with work and working people.

Bread and Roses became my own ideology, my own reason, my own path.

I worked alongside Moe for many years. Being with him was to listen and to learn. And, of course, to talk. Conversation was his way of life, and mine too. It was through talking that he convinced, that he plotted and planned, that he won and he lost, over and over again. He was a person who didn't believe in the word NO, and I too came to believe that NO was an unfortunate concept that could be overruled.

A tireless fighter for working people and for culture, Moe lived in a way that involved figuring out how to make living better for large numbers of people, particularly those in his union, District 1199. They were largely low-wage workers, mostly women, who worked in hospitals, whose job it was to take care of other people. Moe's job was to take care of them by giving them art: theater, music, beautiful posters.

At a certain point, although it's not a clear moment, not a day or a month or even a year, I started creating programs of my own; coming up with my own ways to illustrate bread, and to generate roses of infinite varieties, and then to add as many roses as I could to every struggle. Those roses took many forms. Beautiful posters were my most common effort because, in a very basic way, beauty is both inspiration and hope. We all need beauty on our walls, no matter where those walls are, no matter what our walls look like. I have always known, intuitively, that life is better with beauty, and that beauty has many forms. Calendars and theater performances, writing classes, storytelling, and even poems are ways of providing roses, ways of showing that culture is a benefit that everyone deserves.

Unseenamerica was one of the programs I started; a way for workers and immigrants and unemployed people to tell their stories in their own voices, from their own perspective. The idea was to create a visual history by those inside that history, showing what life really looked like. Showing what people, everyday people, actually see, and what they think of what they see. Thousands of photographers, from migrant workers to nannies, were part of union-sponsored classes. Their pictures, their visions, and their lives became part of a visual historical archive, and were shared in hundreds of exhibits in as many places as we could find, from the U.S. Department of Labor in Washington, D.C., to city halls and classrooms.

Partnering with WDI about 10 years ago was another fortunate and unexpected path. A gifted young photographer, Zoeann Murphy, sat next to me at an information lunch one day. She wanted to use her art form for the greater good, to make the world a little better.

Zoeann came to work at Bread and Roses, in the unseenamerica program. She taught classes and helped photographers and teachers. We eventually worked together with WDI throughout New York State, and helped working people capture their lives through their pictures. The pictures were shown in one of the most visited exhibits at the New York State Museum in Albany, an exciting launch created by WDI, in order to showcase how workers see our lives. This led to WDl launching The Art of Labor, an inspired statewide effort to generate working stories, in many different ways.

When I left Bread and Roses a few years ago, I wanted to be able to provide more roses, to keep planting what I could, around the State of New York, as well as around the country.

With WDI, I was lucky to be able to continue planting and creating roses, and to continue to envision ways for working people around the state to tell their stories, in all the ways we can imagine.

# WE ARE OUR BROTHERS' KEEPERS

Pat Costello

In the course of my lifetime, expenditures—for food, clothing, housing, education, healthcare, transportation, and everything else for my family and me—have been paid for by wages provided and protected by a collectively bargained union contract. I have been truly blessed. This is my story....

Frank Collins was born in 1886 and died in 1980. He was my grandfather. I would like to share a story about my grandfather, and a very important lesson that he taught me as a young man. My grandfather was a retired pipefitter and was 94 years old when he taught me this lesson. This was one of many lessons that he taught me, as he was a very unusual and interesting man. He had a great sense of humor, and taught me that we should find the humor in our day-to-day lives.

A good example of this: He would have a yearly bet with his backyard neighbor about who could grow the biggest tomatoes. My grandfather would painstakingly cut out pictures of red, ripe tomatoes from magazines and tape them to his green tomatoes in just such a way that when his neighbor looked over the fence, it appeared that his tomatoes were already red and ripe, while the neighbor's were still green and growing. He was constantly doing things like that. Never a dull moment!

I rented an apartment from him while I was an apprentice electrician. After work, I would come home and we would sit on the porch, have a few beers, and he would ask about what happened on my jobsite. I think it was his way of staying connected to the construction industry. On this one day, I noticed that he was not chewing tobacco—a habit he had picked up when he was eight years old, and which continued every day his whole life. So I said, "Gramps, how come you're not chewing tobacco?" to which he said, "It just didn't taste good," and that he just might quit! This was a shock; he had a chew in his mouth almost his whole life. He then went on to tell me that he wasn't feeling all that great, and thought he would go to bed—it was 5:30 p.m.

The next day he did not feel much better when I went to work. When I came home, he said that I should take him to the hospital, as he was feeling worse. I put him in my car and started driving to the hospital. He stopped me as I backed out of the driveway and told me to go through downtown Utica— the long way to the hospital. I told him that the other way was shorter, but, as only a 94-year-old man can, he said, "Just be quiet and do what I tell you." So we went the long way. We had just gotten downtown, when he said, "Slow down, I want to show you the building where I installed a boiler in the 1930s." We then traveled only about 100 yards from that building, when he said, "I put a sprinkler system in that building." Building after building, he made me either stop or slow down, as he described what work he had performed there. It was then that it dawned on me that this was his last ride in a car, and he wanted to share his life's work with me. I cried most of that ride as we stopped at dozens of buildings. My grandfather died a few days later. I think about that ride often and share it with our young apprentices. How blessed is a man who can show his grandson, proudly, what he has accomplished in his life, and how blessed was I to have him explain it to me. The lesson: Whatever you choose to do with life, take pride in your work, do it to the very best of your ability, do it with laughter, and do it in a way that you would be proud to show your grandson or granddaughter on your last ride in a car.

My name is Pat Costello and I am 62 years old and, as my old friend Bernie Flaherty, from Cornell, would say, "The shadows of my career are lengthening." I have held various offices and titles for over 35 years in the International Brotherhood of Electrical Workers (IBEW). My perception of what a good labor leader looks like has changed over the span of my career. I will try to explain how my style and passion for representing working men and women was developed.

What has never changed in my mind is that, from the very first office I held as a member of the Joint Apprenticeship and Training Committee (JATC), I took the role of representing other workers as a distinct honor.

Like most of us, my thoughts on many issues were developed as a child, and were a learned reaction to what my parents believed. I was very blessed to have been raised, along with my sister Diane and my brother Dennis, by a very caring Irish family. It is important to mention that they were Irish because, as in most Irish families, my father thought he ran the show, but I learned at a very early age that it was my mother who was the glue, the engine that made our family function.

My father was a union pipefitter, and held many offices in his local union, including being elected president for 12 years. He was a very unapologetic, pro-labor, pro-worker, outspoken advocate for his members. He was as stubborn as any person I have ever met when it came to workers' rights and ways to benefit working families. So, at my dinner table, as a young boy I heard my dad talk about these issues daily.

I will give you two examples of my father's outlook. One had to do with the meat cutters union in our area. They went out on strike for some nine weeks when I was about eight years old. As with most families in the early '60s, we had a very small freezer on top of our refrigerator. When my dad heard about the butchers and meat cutters going on strike, he filled our freezer with meat, enough for about two meals. Yet, during the strike, we did not eat meat. I remember asking my parents why we couldn't have a cookout like our neighbors.

My dad and mom sat me down and explained that the unionized workers whom we bought our meat from were having problems with their owners. And that the workers had tried to bargain for more money and better working conditions. I remember them treating me (remember, only eight years old) like I was an adult when they explained the meat cutters' situation to me. I got it. We ate mac and cheese, grilled cheese, and other meatless meals for the duration of the strike. To this day, the best hamburger I ever had was the first one after they had settled their contract.

The second example is from when my dad's own union went out on strike, as there was a disagreement about their contract. There were a few issues that caused the stalemate, but the big one was an increase in the hourly rate. The two sides of this disagreement were a nickel apart! The strike lasted three months. Our family's reserve funds—our savings account—was depleted. My dad would tell me that, as important as the nickel per hour was, it was just as important that the contractors respected the work done by his members.

He looked at their inability to concede to the nickel raise as a sign of disrespect to the trade. As a side note, I recall our butcher helping us during the strike. He extended credit to my dad, who paid the bill after the strike concluded. Two lessons learned: We are all in this together; the plumber and the butcher, the teacher and the electrician, and the policeman and the nurse, and all of us working people need to help each other succeed; and management needs to respect the efforts and the work performed by its employees.

As I said earlier, my mother held our household together during the good and bad times. She was quiet but displayed every bit as much strength as my dad did. My respect for strong women can be attributed to my mother's quiet strength. My wife, Patricia Ann (McNally) Costello, has displayed all the attributes of my mother in running our household and in raising our four children, Kimberly, Lindsey, Ryan, and Kerry. So I have been in constant contact with strong, capable, and caring women my whole life. It is from that background that I have developed a real appreciation for what women can bring to the workplace—any workplace. I take great pride in the fact that more women are not only entering into the construction field, but are thriving in our industry. I have hated the phrase "non-traditional employees" my whole adult life, and am very happy that I do not hear that phrase much anymore.

Organized labor should be very proud—I know I am—of the fact that, on our worksites, women are paid equal to men when performing the same work. Our collective bargaining agreements do not have different pay for women and men. Women are not paid 70 cents on the dollar as they are in some non-union worksites. This should be a source of pride for us in the labor movement.

Early in my career, I witnessed what I would now call "the old school of labor leaders." They were the table-bangers, the shouters, the kinds of people who had no problem telling the other side of the table to go to hell. As a young man, I thought that was the only way to accomplish anything of importance for our members. These leaders (my mentors) were, in my eyes, giants in our industry. They were responsible for great strides, not only in wages, but in worksite safety, and improvements in our fringe benefits, such as pension, annuity, and healthcare. They were what made the labor movement great. I started out just like them. It took me a while to notice that some of the tactics used by my mentors were no longer as effective as they had once been. While I have never, to this day, eliminated the ability, if needed, to tell the other side to "go to hell," I rarely use it. This is in no way a sign of disrespect to those whom I have followed. Those leaders used what worked. They forged the benefits and working conditions that we enjoy today. We in organized labor will always be indebted to them.

I have changed the way I approach negotiations and represent workers over my career. Today, more than ever, I try to understand what the other side is proposing. I realize that there needs to be a profit margin for them to remain relevant in their industry. I then try to weigh their concerns with what our members need to remain in the middle class and to live their version of the American dream. Most times, the two sides, at the beginning of the process, are miles apart. I have always found that there is some middle-ground we can agree to. Once we establish that, we can chip away at our differences and ultimately reach an agreement that our members can ratify and management can agree to.

In my employment area, we have enjoyed a very good labor/ management relationship with our contractor partners. "Partners" is the key word in that sentence. If they don't prosper, my members do not work. I realize that now more than ever. However, they do not need to "over-prosper." It is our role as labor leaders to make sure that our members receive their fair share of the profits. I think that we in the unionized building trades do a good job of making sure our members are justly compensated for their efforts.

It is, unfortunately, a different story for too many workers in other industries, where CBOs, CFOs, Boards of Directors, and others have seen astronomical increases in their compensation, while those on the shop floor have been left behind. This problem—pay inequity—has the potential to destroy the America that I grew up in. I think we would all agree that America was at its strongest and most vibrant when we had a prosperous and growing middle class. Those workers were the economic engine that made America the envy of the world.

To reverse the erosion of the middle class is what I see as labor's major challenge. We need to help create an economy that rewards good employers who pay decent wages and benefits. We need to stop the practice of outsourcing our jobs overseas, as we race to the bottom. The list is long—from minimum wage, a fair immigration policy, card check, universal healthcare, fair trade policies, stronger worksite safety rules, pre-K education, veterans care, food issues, and on and on. All of these, and many more, are labor's fight. If not us, who?

Those who have the benefit of collective bargaining need to help those less fortunate, and fight for their ability to either climb into, or remain, in the middle-class. We have an ever-growing number of working poor. Those who work 40 hours a week and still need to apply for food stamps. We have lost millions of young workers who simply cannot find meaningful work. They have lost hope—just about the worst thing that can happen to a worker. Somehow—together—we need to re-establish their hope that they can succeed. When workers lose their ability to dream of a better life for themselves and their families, we all suffer.

So, what can we do? The problems seem overwhelming. How can we make a difference? We start with one person at a time. In my trade, when we get a young man or woman out of the cycle of poverty and welfare, and enter them into our apprentice system, we are not only changing their life, but also the lives of their yet-to-be born children and grandchildren. We are giving them hope where they had none. We help them to dream of something better. When we accomplish this, it is truly the best feeling in the world. We can all help in some way. Each person needs to find their own way to give back, to pay it forward. If we rely on the government or big business to reverse this erosion of the middle-class, I think we will only be fooling ourselves. After all, they have contributed to the problem.

This brings me to labor's political involvement. For 40 years, I have worked on campaigns for candidates who said they had the best interests of working families at heart. I have been disappointed many times, as those for whom we worked so hard seemed to have forgotten those of us in the labor movement. For years, I have heard excuses like, "You don't know how hard it is to get this bill passed," or, "If I stand up for your proposal, I will pay the consequences —I may even lose my committee seat," or, "I voted against your position because I knew it wouldn't pass anyway, so why piss off my colleagues on a loser?" What we need is someone who believes in what we believe in. Who's not worried about what their colleagues might think. Who's more concerned with working people than with corporations. Someone like my father and my early mentors who were unapologetic supporters of anything that helped working men and women. Speaking of my father, he had a great line that I use today to describe a lifelong politician with no real-world (work) experience. He would say, "Look at the dumb bastard; he was born on third and thinks he has hit a triple." He also used this to describe rich kids who took over their dad's company after their father had worked his whole life to build it.

One of the things that I have learned about our elected officials is that we need to educate them with regard to our issues and concerns. To assume that they know our positions on various issues is a mistake. Trust me when I say that our enemies are in their ears telling them their positions, and if we do not make a genuine effort to explain our side, they will end up being against us. We need to ask things of them. Sometimes we assume that they will do the right thing without our asking them to get on board. Our not asking for something somehow translates to them assuming we do not have a position on the issue. They may not be as smart as we would like them to be, but it is our job to educate them at whatever level we can. I had my congressman once tell me that he was shocked at the low level of intelligence in the House of Representatives. He told me it is no Mensa convention when they get together.

Again, my dad would say "a bunch of dumb bastards who were born on third and thought that they had hit a triple."

Another issue that I think we in the labor movement need to continually work on is the membership involvement in our movement. The apathy that I see is like a cancer eroding our ability to not only maintain what we have but also to increase our union density, and it will be the demise of our movement if we do not aggressively address it. During every election cycle, this apathy becomes an issue as we try to enlist volunteers to man phone banks, go door to door, and work on campaigns for our friends. My local union has developed a Membership Development Committee that meets quarterly to address any issue that may come up. We have put captains in place that have groups of 10 to 20 members in their cluster. It is a more modern version of the old "phone tree" system. We utilize Twitter, Facebook, instant messaging, and other technologies to get our message out. I think we do a pretty good job of soliciting volunteers but, as is the case for most local unions, I would like to see more involvement. This election cycle, I have witnessed a phone bank that we conducted for a labor-friendly congressional candidate where we had 25 members participate. As great as that was, the candidate stated he had never seen such a turnout from our union. I could not help thinking about what we could accomplish with 50, 100, 150 volunteers.

We must continue to increase the number of our members who

step up when needed. We must educate our young members on the importance of getting involved, and make them understand that elections have consequences. Their ability to make decent wages, with benefits, depends on their involvement. We need to educate our members so they can comfortably write a letter to the editor or speak publicly at legislative meetings and public forums in order to address labor's position on issues. We need, in some cases, to instill a sense of pride in their union membership. Too often, I see our members not defending their collectively bargained wages and benefits publicly when others blame the union movement for budget deficiencies, a failing economy, foreclosures ... the list goes on and on, and our members do not speak out. They almost seem embarrassed by the wages they earn and the benefits that they enjoy. We need to start playing some offense and stop playing defense. It is not labor's fault that the economy is in the state that it is in. We need to stand up for collective bargaining and all its benefits. We need to expose Wall Street, the banks, poor trade agreements, greedy corporations, and the hundreds of other reasons that have led us to where we are today. It is not now, nor has it ever been, labor's fault. The real problem is not our wages and benefits—which we have earned through years of collective bargaining—but, rather, it is the fact that millions of workers are deprived of a place to bargain their conditions with their employers. All working men and women deserve a voice at the worksite. We should be visibly proud of what we have, and help other workers gain a voice.

As far as advice that I would give a younger member who may be interested in running for union office and representing their coworkers, I would offer the following: Take your role as a union official very seriously (because it is). The decisions you make have real-world ramifications on your members and their families. When a member is wronged, make it right—no matter the effort needed to correct it. No issue is too small to address when your member is in the right. When a member is in the wrong, you must have the courage to tell them they are wrong. Do not file worthless grievances or arbitrations on behalf of members who are in the wrong. Counsel your members who have violated their agreements and help them to see their shortcomings. Getting a member back on the right track through your counseling is every bit as important as defending the member who was treated unfairly by management. Never give a member the "bum's rush" when they want to discuss a problem with you. There are times in our members' lives when their union representative is the only person they feel they can come to in order to talk things out. It may not have anything to do with the contract; maybe all they need is someone who will listen. Do not turn your back on that member when they need you the most.

A few years ago, after the tragic suicide of one of our members, who was only 31 years old, I changed the closing section of our union meetings to read as follows:

"With the business of the present meeting being concluded, I declare this local union duly and legally closed until our next regular meeting, unless specifically called. Until our next meeting, please take care of each other and, remember, we are our Brothers' Keepers. Thank you, Brothers and Sisters."

I believe that all the other nuances that are needed to become an effective practitioner in representing workers can be learned. However, you must enter the field with a firm belief that "We are our Brothers' Keepers."

# GROWING THROUGH WORK

## Rosalie DeFrancesco Drago

I am here to foster a safe common ground where people genuinely connect and thrive. Each person I encounter and each task I engage in, I create a space where people identify and develop their God-given gifts. A place where people share their stories, trade ideas, and are fully engaged so that they and their community prosper mentally, physically, spiritually, and financially.

This is my personal mission statement. These words are written on the inside of my notebook and I read them before I start each day. It is what I hope to achieve at home and at work, which are both part of one life—my life. It is about seeing, being open to, and creating opportunity for myself, for my coworkers, for my clients, for my community, for my husband, and for my children. When I share this mission, people ask, "How are you so clear about your purpose? How did you come up with this?" The answer is that I developed myself, as well as awareness, through my work.

I have always found work to be meaningful, enjoyable, and fulfilling. Having been challenged so often to defend my experience of work, I began to ask myself why it is that I feel this way. How did I come to have this context for work? The fact is that I never expected it to be anything else. Why is that?

## My Roots in Work

I grew up in a working-class town in New Jersey that was a mile square. My mother was the child of Russian-Jewish immigrants, and grew up on Ocean Parkway in Brooklyn. My father was the child of second-generation Italian immigrants, and was a World War II veteran. Both my parents believed firmly that work builds one's character, and they relied on work for survival. Note that I say "survive" and not "thrive." We lived just shy of poverty, and the focus was on making ends meet.

My mom was a teacher's assistant in a nursery school four blocks from our home, from the time I was in kindergarten until I left home for college. She did this so she could be home when I got back from school, make dinner, and take care of my father and me every night. When I asked if she liked her job, she would say, "I get to work with children, make art, help pay the bills, and be there to take care of you and your father. What's not to like?"

My father worked as a manager at a local manufacturing company and, later, in the real estate business. When asked if he liked his job, he always replied emphatically, "Yes. It is a new adventure every day."

Being of limited means, he would secure work at factories that produced items that we needed. When my mom and dad were first married, he worked at a linen factory. When I was a small child, he worked at Gabrielle Toys.

Dad would seek out a manufacturer that he wanted to work for and then comb through the papers or stop by to find out if there was a position open. For a few days in a row, he would visit the facility and watch the workers. He would have lunch where they had lunch and listen to them talk about work; what they liked, what they disliked, how things could be better. He would sometimes engage them in conversation and ask questions. Then he would scribble a whole bunch of revisions to his résumé, and my mom would retype it (on the typewriter!). The next day, he would go back and submit it. When he interviewed, he had a good understanding of the work and issues on the floor. When he was hired (and he had a 95% success rate), he would work to address the issues and implement the suggestions that he heard from the workers.

Around the time I was in second grade, he switched careers. My parents borrowed from family members in order to send me to private school, hoping to give me a better life, but our family needed more money to manage each month. After some discussion, my parents figured that if my dad could be the superintendent of a building, we could live rent-free. A former army man, he was able to fix anything. He took a semester of courses and got the necessary licenses, and then went door to door to local buildings. When he found one that was both hiring and suitable for habitation by my mother's standards, he used the same approach he used with the manufacturers: visited the building, spoke to residents about the facility, and then applied to the management company. He was hired, and we moved into a one-bedroom apartment in the building within a week.

My experience of work has been that it is a vehicle to obtaining what you need and want, as well as a place to learn about life. It is there for you, accessible, if you are willing to explore and risk a bit.

Work was also a source of joy and comfort. It was part of my family life, not a separate thing. I associate work with times where I laughed and played and created memories with my family. We worked at home together, cleaning off the table after dinner, washing and putting the dishes away. We'd clean the house together on weekends, inside and out. (Dad sawed the handle down to the right size on the broom and the rake so I could help.) "Time to do our work!" my parents would exclaim with joy, making a game out of it.

When my dad needed to fix a part for something, he would find something for me to fix too. We'd set our tools out on the table. I took apart and reassembled the alarm clock and radio countless times. (I do not claim that they actually worked afterwards). When my mother cooked, she would give me a job to do, even when I was two: snapping the ends off string beans, taking peas out of the pod, scrubbing vegetables. They never sent me off to watch TV or play while there was work to be done.

My favorite thing to do was going to work with my father, and my fondest memories of him are from the times I did. When he worked at Gabrielle Toys, he would take me onto the floor and introduce me to each worker. As we walked to each of their stations, he would tell me a little about them; if they had a child my age, where they came from. They would greet me and explain what they were doing, and I would watch the toys I played with being made.

I experienced work as fulfilling, both emotionally and physically, way before I ever got paid for it.

### My Road to Work

Frustrated by all the negative responses I got because of my family's financial position, I asked to get a "real job" (not babysitting) when I was 14. I asked my father for advice, since I didn't know what I wanted to do and had no experience. My father said, "You gain experience and knowledge through work. To get a job and be good at it, you have to find out what you don't know and where to get that information—just observe, listen to people, and ask questions." We spent a Saturday afternoon walking around our town retail center and discussing all the different types of jobs; what I thought would be involved and what I thought I might like or be good at. We settled on a small cookie factory, and my parents helped me apply.

After the cookie factory, I worked part-time throughout high school. I was a cashier and informal manager at the local 7-Eleven at age 15, a cashier at the supermarket when I was 16, and delivered pizza when I was 17. When it came time to apply to college, I wanted to go to school for journalism and media arts. My guidance counselor said it was a waste of time and not practical but helped me work on my applications anyway. I started college at a local four-year school and lived on campus. I worked in retail and started waiting tables to pay for tuition.

My dad got sick after my first semester, so I left school and came home to help out. I found an apartment nearby, worked two jobs, and was home every day to help out and help take care of my dad. One of my jobs was waiting tables on the weekends at a café in Weehawken, along the Hudson River. One day, a regular customer, an older gentleman who drove an antique Jaguar, asked me to sit and talk to him. My manager told me to "sit and listen to what he says." The older gentleman asked me, if I could have any car I wanted, what it would be. I said a '69 Camaro. He asked, why not a BMW. I told him it was because I didn't have that kind of money and couldn't live that kind of lifestyle. He said, "Only because you say so." He went on to describe an experiment that he and a colleague had conducted. They placed an ad in the classifieds with the same job description for three months in a row—each month, they changed the salary. First $30K, then $60K, then $90K.

He went on to explain that they never got the same résumés, and asked me, "If you thought you had the qualifications and experience to do the job at $30K, why wouldn't you apply at $90K? Because people are like cadavers with a tag on their toe. The tag says 'I am worth this much,' and they live their whole lives, and make all their choices, based on that number." I went back to my shift distracted.

I remembered all the times my parents and I walked past houses and imagined what it would be like to live in one, all the "what if" conversations, and all the infuriating "we can't" conversations. The next week, I walked up to the old gentleman's table and said, "Please tell me how to change my life." He handed me *Think and Grow Rich!* by Napoleon Hill. For the next few weeks, we discussed the book after my shift. One day, he handed me a newspaper classified ad. Then he said, "There is a job open at the main office in Customer Service for the company that owns this restaurant. Why don't you apply?" I told him I didn't have a suit. He gave me $100, and told me to go buy one and pay him back when I got the job and my first paycheck. I called, scheduled an interview, bought the suit, got the job, and paid him back with my first paycheck.

We had one final meeting before I started the job. He said, "If anything were possible, what would you want to accomplish?" I resisted at first, but when he pushed, I said, "$100K salary, a Master's degree, a house, and a best friend to go through life and have a family with." He said, "It's yours. You just have to go and get it." I asked how. He said, "Start by making sure you do work that doubles your salary every four years."

There was that message again. Not knowing how to do something, not knowing anyone—these were not things to be frightened of or let stand in your way. The responsibility to identify and create opportunities was up to me. There was no "right" or "wrong" job. Just another chance.

I started as a customer service representative at NY Waterway in 1994, making $19K. My first office job. I quit my waitressing job and never saw the old gentleman again. My dad died of lung cancer in the fall.

The four years I spent at NY Waterway included two promotions (first to Customer Service Manager, then to Sightseeing Sales Manager) and the beginning of a decade-long career in tourism. I watched, I listened, and I asked questions. I arrived at 7:30 a.m. and had coffee with the VP, ate lunch with the deckhands and bus drivers, stayed late, and worked weekends with my boss. My boss was an extraordinary mentor, who invited me to shadow her everywhere she went: every meeting, every committee, every association. I did everything I could to learn about the tourism industry. This led me to a job as Director of Marketing and Sales at the Intrepid Sea, Air & Space Museum. At this point, I had begun to serve on many tourism committees and was traveling nationally. Three years later, I joined the Marketing & Communications team at the American Museum of Natural History, and started traveling the world to promote the museum and tourism in New York City. I started chairing committees and planning promotional events for New York City .

One day, when the Museum was working on the Annual Report, the Editorial Department called and asked, "What is your Master's degree in?" I asked them what they meant, since I didn't have one. "Well, what about your BA?" they asked. I told them I didn't have that either. A few minutes later, I got called in by my boss. "I just heard you don't have a four-year degree. It is required in order to work here." "Well, you hired me," I said. Puzzled, we went together to HR and obtained a copy of my résumé, which confirmed that I did not say I had completed college. I was immediately enrolled in a matching tuition program.

I was always fascinated by how our civilizations came to be—
and why they failed—so I went back to school to complete my
Bachelor's degree in Humanities and Classic Civilization. I graduated from Montclair State University in 2000; it took me 11 years.
After three years, a position as Assistant VP of Marketing opened up,
and I applied. My boss took me aside and said that, as a result of my
educational experience, I would not be considered, and that, in order
to advance, I would have to go somewhere else.

So I did. For a year, I worked for a global entertainment company as Vice President of Marketing at Madame Tussauds. Working
with a cohort across seven countries, developing branding and corporate culture locally and regionally—it was like getting an MBA.
I remember my very first meeting, where the people in the Finance
Department told me I would have to write a complete marketing plan
and budget, and that my compensation would be based on hitting
revenue goals after Earnings Before Interest, Depreciation and Amor-
tization (or EBITDA). I had no idea what that meant, but I spent
days on the phone and in meetings, and a sleepless weekend writing
the plan and budget. I watched, I listened, I learned. It was there that
I witnessed the most impactful and engaged workforce I had ever
seen. The General Manager shared the entire budget line-by-line with
the entire staff, and explained that if they could help reach revenue
and cut cost, they would have wage increases and bonuses. The staff
worked like crazy, generated innovative solutions, and managed their
own schedules, to the great success of the organization. I loved the
fact that management understood that the people, the ground-level
people, were always the heart of the organization.

It was a tremendous learning experience, yet I didn't feel like
I fit in. In a frank discussion with the General Manager, she said I
cared too much about people and not enough about profit, and that
I was better suited to work for a non-profit or in public service.
Searching my soul, I realized she was right.

Having an interesting, well-paying career, finishing college,
serving on industry committees, and traveling the world was a long

way to come for someone like me. Having evidence that I could do well and like my job gave me the confidence and permission to start seeking out what I cared about. Work led me to a deep curiosity and interest in the impact of our economic development initiatives in New York City's neighborhoods—the people, the businesses, the places. I started to reach out and offer my experience and expertise as a consultant, and had the great privilege of writing the Strategic Plan and Tactical Handbook for Brooklyn Tourism for then-borough president Marty Markowitz in 2002, which led me deeper and deeper into Brooklyn's neighborhoods.

In 2004, my mom called me from the hospital. She was having trouble breathing. I drove from Brooklyn to New Jersey, and within a few hours we learned that she had lung cancer, which had already spread through her body. Nineteen days later, I watched her take her last breath. During her last few days, she said, "I always told you to be careful, be responsible, don't take too much risk or you might get hurt. I was wrong. Risk everything and live with your heart."

I spent the next year working as a consultant in Brooklyn, trying to listen to my heart. This was no longer simply a good idea, this heart thing. For me, it was life or death. I was no longer working to put poverty behind me—I was working to create a life worth living. It was here that I made a tremendous shift. While I believed I could create the opportunities to find value in my work, I was now able to find work that reflected my values.

I attended several local meetings and heard the then-president of the Brooklyn Chamber of Commerce speak on numerous occasions. He was smart and passionate about building a better Brooklyn. He related with equal measure to the maintenance staff and elected officials. I admired him greatly and shared his passion for the borough. I approached him after a meeting and told him I was committed to helping him realize his vision for Brooklyn, and asked how I could work with him. I offered all my tourism and marketing expertise in return for a chance to learn economic development in depth. He created a position for me as a consultant, which then evolved into Vice President of Marketing & Membership at the

Brooklyn Chamber of Commerce, where, among many things, I got to work with Brooklyn manufacturers to promote their products. I attended every meeting, read every book, and learned all I could about economic development.

Working at something I loved, with a team of people I deeply respected, made all things seems possible. I met the man I was meant to spend my life with. We planned our wedding. It was 2008 and the market crashed. We got married, then both lost our jobs and our savings, while also having a brand new baby on the way. My husband couldn't secure work for two years. I took on consulting jobs; working on neighborhood economic development projects and helping small-business owners organize to create the communities they envisioned together. In our one-bedroom apartment in Brooklyn, we welcomed Michael John in December of 2009; Madeline arrived two months after I completed my graduate degree in 2012.

In my application essay to NYU, I wrote about the way in which we approach economic development, and how we develop these plans for communities, centered on buildings and attracting businesses to a space. Building structures without building a community is fruitless. I said I wanted to invest my time, my experience, and my heart in changing that. In essence, I wanted everyone to have the opportunities I had.

So here I am—filled with gratitude and deeply blessed. I escaped poverty and made my dreams come true. Fulfilling the commitment made that fateful day in the restaurant, I doubled my salary every four years—I earned a promotion that got me a salary that once seemed unattainable in 2008 before I lost my job. I was (and still am) fortunate to have people in my life who called me to a higher game, and that I was open and willing to answer their call.

I feel truly blessed and grateful for every minute. Now, as a mother of two small children, my actions and attitudes lay the foundation that will set them on their own paths. How do I create the same love of work I have and instill in them the expectation that they can author their future?

Oliver Wendell Holmes penned: "To reach the port of heaven

one must sail. Sometimes with the wind, sometimes against it. Always sail, never drift nor lie at anchor."

For me, this means to really choose a direction and be invested in it with all your heart. To learn what you can, and to be open and engaged during the journey. If you are, then you can feel the wind shift, and you know how and where it is time to alter or adjust your course.

I remember the birthday when I received my first toy chest. I loved it, and called it my Treasure Chest. It was beautiful, but it was also empty. When my father worked at Gabrielle Toys, he brought home toys for me. When he left that job, the chest was full— full of beautiful things that I played with every day, and cherished.

Work has been that for me. I was an empty chest when I started working. Each job was an adventure, full of hidden treasure. Just like that chest in my childhood bedroom, I didn't know what would be in it when it would come, but I knew it would be filled. Through my work, I filled that chest with experience, knowledge, confidence, and pride. It connected me to others and to myself. It developed my skills and taught me who I am, through trial and error and through individual practice and reflection. It gave me freedom. It helped me hear my heart and discover my purpose.

Work is the joyful discovery of who we are and what we can become. If you are connected to it, it shows you clearly where you are in your development, and leads you to where you are meant to be. It is a hearth for the fire that burns inside you.

# THE THREE-INCH MIRROR

Mary Jo Ferrare

You can hear the chanting Friday afternoons during lunch hour. Curiously Gregorian in tone and inflection, the voice of the Muezzin pierces Utica's downtown section with the call to prayer, the *Adhan*. "Praise Be To Allah." Amplified from the rooftop, the bullhorn beckons solemnly. Looking up, I am reminded at once of the air raid drills of my youth and the shattering vibration of the B-52s circling Griffiss Air Force Base. I would cover my ears and run inside. It was that loud.

Beneath the mosque's white stucco facade stands the brick-and-mortar structure of the Central United Methodist Church. Its parishioners long dispersed to the suburbs, the church remained vacant for years, a relic of the city's heyday. Placed on the county dole and slated for demolition, it was purchased at the eleventh hour by the Bosnian Islamic Association. Now, minarets peek from the roof and the crescent moon and star welcomes Muslims. A singular comfort, I imagine, for them as well as for me. They worship as one, and I recognize faith, repurposed in a holy place.

Changes come at us in rapid-fire succession, dizzying on the heels of a decline which consumed a generation of workers, and culminating with the Great Recession. In that monumental avalanche of loss, entire industries evaporated and, with them, livelihoods were extinguished. For those of us in the field of workforce development, it was an eternity of hand-wringing helplessness. We witnessed the vast number of 40- and 50-somethings who banked on retiring from Oneida Limited, ConMed, Rite Aid, Covidien, Daimler Bus Industries, and other companies, a*d nauseam.* Dismissed by corporate America and minimized in contemporary culture, this is one population anxious for redemption and intrigued by the potential. They navigate the world of online job applications carefully, incredulously. "Why wouldn't I deliver my résumé in person?" I'm asked. "How else is the employer going to recognize me?"

We forge ahead now, re-energized, our grace period steadily ticking away. Tasked with realigning the strengths of a region etched in industrial manufacturing, we pledge to fulfill the promise of the New World Order. To Utica's north rises the Computer Chip Commercialization Center, or Quad-C, the long-awaited savior, its go-ahead stalled for over a decade in a bureaucratic stalemate reaching all the way to the office of the Commander in Chief. Construction of the Quad-C, currently in the second of three phases on the SUNY Poly campus, has harnessed the region in a whirlwind of anticipation. The excitement is palpable to bystanders, students, and building trades workers alike. Those of us whose knowledge of nanoscale science lies on the periphery nevertheless recognize it as essential to the technology hierarchy, particularly as an increasing number of occupational sectors rely on high-performance electronic and transistor devices.

One such venture is being championed at the Griffiss Business and Technology Park, 15 miles to the west, where the FAA has approved testing to determine how best to integrate commercial and civil unmanned aerial systems (UAS) into the national airspace system. Wildly innovative and futuristic, the positioning of civilian drones at Griffiss International is causing a ruckus of both controversy and glee. Looming large is the absence of any regulatory provisions which would enforce the protection of civil liberties, particularly those dealing with privacy rights. The FAA claims it possesses no jurisdiction over the matter but mandates that each of the six selected U.S. trial sites develop individual standards to better formulate such policy going forward. Opponents, however, cite the need for such legislation prior to testing, and one can hardly dismiss their concerns.

The reality of data-collecting surveillance, transmitted via small airborne cameras to civilian computer feeds, fuels a culture already hopped-up on healthy doses of paranoia. Big Brother ascends.

Meanwhile, armed with strategic vigor, UAS proponents advocate for drone use in the private sector. They refer to specific industries where access is often problematic and costly. Aerial imaging and processed data, utilized to monitor crop growth and weather trends in remote areas, could better inform the environmental and agricultural sectors. Response time in natural disaster occurrences would be maximized, expediting search and rescue efforts in ravaged communities. These and other benefits to health and human welfare seem undeniable, yet they could realistically be overshadowed by the escalation of for-profit drone use. As intriguing as the technology itself, the assortment of potential business applications becomes more mesmerizing with each new iteration. The debate will likely rage on, the implications not fully articulated or understood. But whether one is pro or con, there's no denying the capacity of UAS to alter the dynamics of the workplace as we know it. That the science is being tested locally speaks to the definitiveness of our economic resurrection.

As we begin our courtship of the millennials, we understand that only through the collaborative efforts of many will we attract and retain this cohort. At ease with technology and privy to an all-encompassing worldview, the emergent workforce possesses an unparalleled sophistication. How we meet this level of finesse, particularly as members of an aging community, will ultimately define our success. Economic development professionals' promise of well-paying jobs must be couched in a pulse-reviving social and business culture, a conduit of peer-to-peer communication acting on its own behalf as the best possible information and referral service. We understand the urgency of making this network a reality, and as the community rallies to put on its best renaissance face, we broadcast the desirability factor in hopes of elevating the region's visibility and encouraging the buy-in of the global generation.

A look at revitalization trends in other upscale locales serves as useful examples. One noteworthy indicator is the accessibility to modern housing combining both residential and commercial spaces. Several private investors, in conjunction with the federal Housing and Urban Development Department (HUD), have acted on this knowledge. Three former downtown businesses are currently being converted to contemporary mixed-use space, the most conspicuous being the HSBC Bank, an iconic urban landmark set apart by its Carrarra marble facade and gracefully arched windows scaling from ground level to the third floor. Soon to be home of the Landmarc (hashtag UticaRisesFromHere), the building boasts commercial space at street level (recently leased) with luxury studio and balconied one- and two-bedroom loft apartments occupying the upper floors. Structural steel has been erected on the roof and will support construction of a new dining establishment and after-hours lounge. Mixed-use development, including some loft apartments, is capturing both interest and commitment, and infusing a dose of cosmopolitan living into Utica's inner-city limits.

Oneida County's centuries-old tradition of farming and agriculture also makes us worthy of a second look, particularly as issues regarding food production and safety continue to draw attention. The challenges associated with feeding the world, while also ensuring earth's sustainability, are all part of the ongoing conversation in a global economy. Mired in environmental stewardship, agricultural innovation and new methods of farming have exploded into mainstream consciousness and are at the forefront of the "grow local, eat local" movement. The sale and consummation of fresh, locally raised food products coincide with the reduction of synthetic fertilizers and other potential carcinogens used to preserve exported goods. Advocated by many as the best possible solution for the planet, and wholly embraced by the millennial locavores, the promise and popularity of this movement is evidenced locally by the development of several community-based gardens. They appear as a series of strikingly long, rectangular raised beds in vacant lots spaced throughout the city's older residential district, in neighborhoods known for questionable activity.

The gardens came into existence initially as a pilot program offered through the Oneida County Department of Health, which sought to provide an alternative to traditional planting in soil contaminated with lead-based paint. The program was soon embraced by several non-profit organizations and a few generous small-business owners, who donated both manpower and building materials. Met with curiosity and support from civic-minded onlookers, the gardens have been remarkably well-received. Food, it appears, serves as the most legitimate of common denominators, starting conversations and transcending both socioeconomic class and social status. The presence of the gardens, cultivating both fresh vegetables and new relationships, is urban renewal at its finest; the unification of labor and capital for the betterment of the community.

Nontraditional agriculture has also provided an avenue of workforce development for one of our most difficult-to-place populations: Limited English Proficient (LEP) adult refugees. Many of these individuals were employed in warehouse and assembly positions where no English was required, and lost their jobs during the financial crisis. Since then, collaborative and prolonged efforts to assist them in overcoming language and literacy barriers have been frustrating and mostly unsuccessful. The implementation of the community gardens is helping to change that, as we learn to maximize the strengths of this significant and valuable cohort.

Formal training in contemporary horticultural practices (a 10-week pilot program, facilitated in English and interpreted in a variety of languages) has been particularly beneficial to the Somali, Bantu, Burmese, and other agrarian-based groups. The wide-ranging curriculum, presented in both classrooms and field settings, covers specific food systems and three-season maximization of plant and plant-type yields in Upstate New York. Modern farming techniques and fresh food sale regulations are taught, as well as basic marketing and interpersonal communication skills. For the capstone event, program graduates are assisted in setting up and staffing a "food sale stall" at the Oneida County Public Market, as well as other local fresh food venues. Utilized in conjunction with the 155 raised-bed

Unity Garden project, the horticulture certificate initiative increases self sustainability and promotes microenterprise in a population categorically marginalized and considered one of the least likely to gain economic independence. One step forward, one small measure of success.

Our region's rich tradition of production is emphasized by a generational scope of work covering the agricultural, manufacturing, and building trades sectors. The value of working with one's hands, minimized for decades in American culture, has enjoyed resurgence due, in no small part, to the artisans, craftsmen, and creators who embody the do-it-yourself spirit. Entrepreneurship, the transformation of an idea into a value-added enterprise, is the perfect vehicle for resourceful individuals (and like-minded collaborators) who put their talents to work with the goal of effecting economic, social, and intellectual progress. The discovery and application of entrepreneurial solutions to pressing societal issues is a fundamental challenge posed to local college students and supported through Mohawk Valley Community College and SUNY Poly. With the establishment of the Community Entrepreneurship thINCubator and Innovation Challenge New York, these higher-education institutions have created an innovation platform which will launch the best hands-on ideas of our youth and be instrumental in the pursuit of an ever-improving quality of life for all.

It's a long-standing joke in our family: the son, a serial class cut-up, barely makes it out of high school and is steered, in parental desperation, to join the military. He enlists in the U.S. Navy and moves up and out of the ranks to become a nuclear engineer. The daughter, a seriously introverted "A" student and college shoe-in, chooses instead to pursue a career in the building construction trades, mystifying many but ultimately ensuring a third generation of skilled union labor. Not exactly the prescribed course, yet, seldom have I regretted the decision. Most of my career choice requirements were fulfilled by strenuous and pure work that was production-oriented and constantly in flux. The trades soothed an inherent craving for the outdoors, a fix I need to satisfy to this day. As a member of the Laborers' International Union of North America (LIUNA #35), I engaged in nearly every aspect of commercial building construction, from the excavation and pouring of foundation footings to the final "punch list," a series of finish work tasks completed prior to new owner(s) taking possession of a building.

It was a terrific education. The nature of the industry places workers in a revolving door of jobsites, with each location being unique in its particular size and scope of work. Constructing additions and/or completing renovations to existing facilities positioned us in the daily operations of a specific business, corporate, or industrial culture. We were privy to a wealth of inside information, and met interesting groups of employees from all walks of life. Many individuals I met were long-term employees, "lifers," who possessed few options to upgrade their skills or access career-advancement opportunities. Plugged in to one or two job tasks, the majority seemed resigned, content even, with their status. They existed in a seemingly satisfying plateau of inertia, which always made me want to ask questions. I was curious to hear their stories. They were often equally curious to hear mine. In retrospect, I understand how those personal exchanges, years of them, broadened my conceptualization of work, and laid bare both the complexities and complacencies of human nature. Although the work I was doing was often merciless, I considered myself fortunate. I knew I would be moving on to another job at a new location, with an entirely different cast of characters. Working in the trades had its distinct advantages.

I don't recall making a conscious decision to pursue a formal education. It was, rather, a gradual realization of the years going by, the physical demands of my occupation, and a quiet, persistent, and personal dissatisfaction that I couldn't name. A friend encouraged me to test the waters by registering for Utica College's 10-month Paralegal Certificate Program. It was good advice. The following year, I returned to UC and enrolled in my first two credit-bearing courses.

It seemed inconceivable to me that I would ever attend Hamilton College. The school was prestigious and selective, and its tuition took my breath away. But the moment I heard about Hamilton's program for "returning" students, I knew I wanted in. Admitted on a trial basis for two semesters, I attended classes as a non-matriculated, part-time student. Shortly thereafter, I was accepted as a second-semester sophomore. In that instant, I realized I was going to gamble my life's savings, but it hardly mattered. I thought of Karl Wallenda, the great German-American high-wire artist, and a quote that resonated with me: "Life is on the wire, everything else is just waiting."

The best education, I believe, is the one that changes the way you think. The six years I spent "on the hill" were among the most illuminating of my life. As a Women's Studies major, I learned how history and culture perpetuate traditional gender roles, and why my experiences in the building trades were reflective of a larger social movement to dismantle the patriarchal stronghold. It makes sense to me now that occupations most closely associated with masculinity are the ones facing the longest and loudest denial from the general populous. I wish I had known that going in, but I know it now, and the understanding makes all the difference.

My family flew in from all points to attend Hamilton College's commencement. Through laughter and tears, we agreed that the phrase "better late than never" had never held so much meaning. I remember the pomp and circumstance, the sound of the bagpipes, the look on my father's face. I knew something good was coming, and it did, in the shape of a second career, which gave me the freedom to utilize my knowledge in service to others.

Recently, a coworker presented me with a miniature hand-held silver-plated mirror. On the back of it is an engraving: John A. Roberts & Co. Utica, New York 1911. I later learned that Roberts & Co. was a downtown department store renowned for both its selection of fine textiles and its elegant fifth-floor Tea Room. According to a September 1911 edition of the *Syracuse Herald Journal*, Roberts & Co. was "The Store of a Thousand Wonders, Utica's Foremost Showplace Outside of New York City—the Greatest Department Store in the State." The mirror was given to shoppers during the Christmas rush that year as a token of appreciation. I forwarded the information to my colleague. "What are the chances," she laughed, "of finding something like that in a Vermont flea market the size of two football fields?"

I did some further research on the store's namesake. A Remsen native and lifelong resident of the Mohawk Valley, Roberts was a successful entrepreneur who possessed a deep interest in community welfare. He invested his energies directly into the city, where he was a charter member of the Utica Chamber of Commerce and Oneida Historical Society. According to A History of the *Mohawk Valley: Gateway to the West* reference collection at Schenectady County Public Library, Roberts's career was closely intertwined with the early growth and development of the city in the early 20th century: "The achievements of John A. Roberts carried with them an impetus to the advancement of Utica as a center of business for Central New York. He built for the future. His faith in Utica was strong, and today, the great business of John A. Roberts & Company stands as a monument to his vision and faith." Indeed, Roberts was one of many forward-thinking individuals at the cusp of the great economic boom which would define the Mohawk Valley. I have to believe he would be pleased with his department store's legacy: a thriving senior housing complex still serving a purpose in the community he so valued.

United by generations of workers who sought the right to a living wage and enjoyed the privilege of upward mobility, our history remains a source of regional pride and ownership. How we distinguish ourselves going forward will likely be measured in much the same way: by the contributions of our incumbent, foreign-born, and newly entered workforce taking precedence in the emerging occupational landscape. Innovation will change them and they will alter the meaning of the word. It is a vortex of promise, enriched by the past, fluid in the present, inseparable from the future. In the exhilarating midst I'm caught; one foot in, the other one ready. I reach for the mirror, tucked away in my pocket, as I climb the steps to the State Office Building and go back to work.

# WORKING STORIES

# OUR COLLECTIVE CONSCIENCE

## Andrea D. Goldberger

*Labor cannot stand still. It must not retreat. It must go
on, or go under.*    —Harry Bridges

I see this young woman again and again. Her name is Andrea.
She is listening as her father shares stories from his workday. His
work is done in a grocery store meat room and freezer, the team of
people working together to complete necessary tasks: break down a
side of beef, cut, grind, wrap, package, and fill the case. The additional work her father has taken on as union steward is woven
through the stories. She hears the satisfaction and, at times, the
hardship, this work brings him. Sometimes she is 16 years old, at her
first real job, bagging groceries at Chicago Market; listening to and
supporting Amelia, her cashier, as she pleasantly greets her customers, bringing a smile to those who have had a hard day; must hurry
home to cook dinner, care for a sick child, or prepare for a holiday.
Other times, I see Andrea as a cashier, trained by Amelia to display
her graceful energy, even when her feet hurt. This Andrea is worried
about her grades, paying her bills, or her dad driving to pick her
up from work after his own long workday. Later she is in college,
studying hard while she works part-time to help with expenses. She
understands the importance of education; "college" was her parent's
mantra throughout her school years. She will be the first family

member to graduate from college. Another time, I see her talking to workers about the value of a union job, shopping to feed her own family, and eventually managing union benefit plans. Her children grow into young adults, and she contemplates their futures. Mostly, I see her in the mirror.

When I consider the topic of work and workers in New York State, I naturally think of it within the context of organized labor, since I have worked as a member of, and on behalf of, the labor movement for more than 37 years. I think of the role organized labor has played in the American economy and how unions use our influence to advance all workers.

The literal blood, sweat, and tears of workers laid the foundation for the formation and early growth of labor unions. As organized labor grew in numbers, so did labor's influence. When this influence became strong enough to have an impact on elections, politicians took notice. Democrats began to partner with the labor movement to align their agendas with the interests of workers, hoping to garner labor's support during elections. The culture promoted a coming together of all—corporations and workers alike—to help America prosper. Building the American economy as a world power was our focus, and the foundation for doing so was the creation of an environment that encouraged meaningful job creation and a productive, responsible workforce. With a prosperous American economy as a common goal, elected officials, corporations, and labor worked together to establish legislative initiatives that: (1) incented corporations to create meaningful jobs; (2) developed social programs to assist and uplift workers; and (3) promoted a harmonious relationship between companies and workers. Prosper and grow we did.

Success brought new challenges. As our economy grew, America became a world leader. As companies and workers prospered, a shift in perspective began. With prosperity came a sense of entitlement and complacency. Organized labor worked hard on behalf of its existing members to maintain a standard of living that had been secured over many years. Although some organizing of non-union workers still occurs, the urgency to grow in numbers is not as fierce as it was in earlier days. Many labor leaders believed that taking care of their own members would be a beacon that would draw in non-union workers. With limited resources and the ever-increasing attacks on workers' rights, organized labor fell into a pattern of fighting for worker protections through legislation, which was a benefit for all workers, but did little to promote real growth of unions. Many workers believed that they did not need to unionize, because the government afforded them rights and protections. An "I've got mine" mentality took precedence over helping everyone succeed. Corporations capitalized on this change in environment and promoted a "me" culture, encouraging workers to put their self-interests above those of their coworkers. As this new culture of "selfism" took hold, collectivism became something to be avoided. Accusations of socialism intimidated many. A societal shift occurred, where individualism became the principle. We stopped believing that "it takes a village" and, instead, decided that each should take care of his/her own. Although the labor movement continued to have political and economic influence, this influence was diminished by a continued reduction in the number of unionized workers. This shift took place in corporate America as well, with corporate responsibility to its workers and society taking a back seat to increased profitability and shareholder returns. The result of this cultural shift is a diminishing middle class, with America's wealth now concentrated in just one percent of the population, and more families in poverty than ever before.

I have seniority in the labor movement, and with that comes a heightened sense of insight and responsibility for my, and our, legacy. I ask myself and others, what exactly is the labor movement's role in America and New York State's economy today? A shift in culture is needed to restore the American economy and the standard of living of working families. The labor movement can, and must, facilitate a shift in consciousness by developing and implementing programs focused on collectivism. We must work with elected officials and companies to pass new legislation and strengthen enforcement of existing laws that support and uplift workers and their families. We must develop programs that promote job creation. And we must break down barriers within the labor movement to facilitate a platform in which diverse unions can support and build a culture of collectivism among union members that spills over to the unorganized workforce. Let the change begin.

My parents were first- and second-generation Italian-Americans, my father the second eldest of eight children and my mother the youngest of seven. Growing up through World War II and the post-war recovery, they experienced the economic hardships of those times, as well as the boom of the 1950s. My grandfather, a crane operator, worked hard to support his family, but, as was common, additional income was needed to keep the household running. My grandmother was kept busy raising children. The money brought in by a job overshadowed the value of an education, and so my father left school to join the world of work. From this point forward, his education was obtained through on-the-job training and lessons learned through the experience of work and family. My mother's parents were hardworking immigrants—my grandfather a railroad worker, my grandmother a factory worker. Much younger than her siblings, my mother spent a great deal of time on her own while my grandparents worked. My mother's artistic talent earned her a college scholarship. Today, many parents would be proud of this accomplishment. At that time, my grandfather saw little value in a college degree, let alone an art degree. The value was in a job that provided immediate income, especially for a woman who would likely get married and raise a family. My parents were married in 1960, when they were 21. I am the eldest of their four children.

I was born into organized labor. My father, Joe, was an active union member and steward. Stories about his work and his union colored our lives with a deep understanding that the true value of work and workers is amplified and secured by union membership. One of my father's stories, repeated often, involved his younger self, when he was 17 years old and working in a meat packinghouse. It was back-breaking, messy, potentially hazardous work. A coworker introduced himself as the union steward, and took the time to explain why union dues were coming out of his paycheck and what it meant to work as part of a union. My dad didn't think much more about it, aside from thinking he sure could use that dues money in his pocket. A few months later, this same steward asked to see my dad's paystub. The steward took a look, told my dad that he was due a pay increase as part of the wage progression in his union contract, and promised to take care of it with management. The following week, the raise and back-money owed was in my dad's paycheck. This was a defining moment for my dad: a clear demonstration of the value provided by a union contract, a good union steward, and a union job. When he was laid off from this job, his mission was to secure another job, a union job, in the meat industry.

In 1961, shortly after I was born, my father was laid off from Gold Medal Packing. With the responsibility of a wife and baby, he realized that he needed a sustainable job, a career. Of course, it needed to be union. Every day he walked to the nearby Chicago Markets, a unionized grocery store, and asked whether there were any openings for meat cutters. His persistence paid off five weeks later. The meat department manager was waiting for my father's daily visit and was happy to tell him that the Market had an apprentice meat cutter position open. My father's daily visits were testimony to his reliability as an employee. He advanced from apprentice to journeyman: a respectable career, a union trade. Within a few years, he decided to run for the position of union steward, and was elected by his coworkers. He rewarded their trust in him by conscientiously representing them in grievance meetings and contract negotiations. Recognized as a solid steward and worker activist, he was later nominated and elected to serve on his union's executive board, and then as union staff and an officer. He took pride in his work and in his union. He appreciated that his union job enabled him to support our family, allowed my mom to stay at home to care for us, and provided family healthcare benefits. He was steadfast in his beliefs, and always stood firmly on the side of workers and his union.

My dad passed away in 2003, but his beliefs are reflected in my own each and every day. Thanks to my dad's union pension, union retiree healthcare, and Social Security benefits, my mom is able to maintain the home they shared and is financially self-sufficient.

I became a union member in 1977, working at the same grocery store where my father worked. Amelia took responsibility for me. As a seasoned cashier, she guided me to be focused on the customer, and as a union member, she mentored me. In effect, she saw me as a customer, one whom she served. She took a 16-year-old girl under her wing and taught her—me—how to work. In return, I helped Amelia. She succeeded when I bagged fast and conscientiously, so she could pay attention to the next customer. The company won when we treated customers well and they made Chicago Markets their preferred grocer. Today, a 16-year-old girl might be left adrift, and her company would be complaining that high schools are not preparing students for the workforce and that young boys and girls do not have the soft skills needed to succeed. I did not have those skills either. Amelia mentored me, trained me, helped me gain confidence, and showed me what a good worker is. She exhibited shared responsibility, helping me develop into a stronger partner within the union, a partner with the company, and with our community. We all won because Amelia did not have a self-oriented perspective. The union fought for salary and benefits. We had sound leadership from our union steward, my dad. Our union contract united us as a team, a multigenerational team. Despite our age difference, we became friends. I eventually lost touch with Amelia, but more than 30 years later, we bumped into each other and shared the warmth that was built around mutual respect. She talked about life since retiring in 1993 and I explained that I now worked for the union's benefit funds. At that moment, I realized that our lives still intersect. The pension check she receives each month from the union's pension fund has my signature on it.

Another woman stands out: Maude, who worked at General Hospital of Saranac Lake. We met after I finished college and was working as an organizer for my union. In 1985, I came advocating for these hospital workers to join our union. Our challenge was to bring together a diverse group of workers—dietary, housekeeping, clerical, LPNs, lab technicians, maintenance, nursing assistants—and organize them for union representation. Maude came into the process midway. The energy in the room shifted when she walked in. Although we had not met until that day, many workers had mentioned her name. I paid attention. She brought some skepticism, and I could see that everyone listened as she spoke. She wasn't the highest-ranking employee but was definitely a community leader and asked critical questions. She understood what we wanted to accomplish, and agreed it might be worth the risk to strive for a union. She also knew that such battles in small towns had local consequences. Her questions focused on the future. She wanted to know what would happen if the workers voted for the union and then developed buyer's remorse. "How do we get you out of here?" she asked. This was a crucial moment for a young organizer. Understanding that this was a pivotal moment, and that establishing trust was paramount, I explained the decertification process step by step. I told her that if we didn't do right by her, we would deserve to be expelled. She believed me, and trusted that we had the workers' interests at heart. She was willing to take the risk. Maude was a community thought leader. If she hadn't trusted me, they would not have moved forward.

Worker empowerment and collectivism are the essence of union organizing. As an organizer, my job was to build a relationship between the union and potential members. The foundation of this relationship is trust. Developing this relationship only occurs through strengthening the relationships between workers to encourage collectivism. Achieving union representation is a result of the worker empowerment that comes from knowing "we are not one, but many." Maude and I became close friends as we worked together to gain union representation for the hospital workers. We became family in the years to follow when I served as union representative for these workers, guiding them through contract negotiations and the resolution of hundreds of grievances. Our relationship continued after I moved on to other positions within the union and Maude served on the union's executive board. When Maude retired, our regular contact lessened, but our connection did not. In June 2012, I was passing through Maude's hometown and felt compelled to visit her.

She was sitting on her back porch when I pulled into her driveway. She watched as I walked toward her, and her expression was one of pure delight when I said her name. Despite her declining health, she still possessed that unmistakable intelligent sparkle in her warm eyes. A long embrace opened the visit. We shared updates on our children, her grandchildren, and other people we both knew. We reminisced about old times—becoming acquainted as organizing partners, growing a friendship, and working together as union sisters. Soon after this visit, Maude passed away. At her memorial service, I spent time with her family. They all knew of me from Maude's union stories, and embraced me as one of their own. Our connection lives on.

My father, Amelia, and Maude represent who I am and want to be. At this stage of my career, I no longer bag groceries, organize stores and hospitals, or run education and training programs. I am the union's benefits director. I have fiduciary responsibilities. There are a lot of numbers in my job, dollar signs, laws, rules, regulations, and reports. There is one primary responsibility: Amelia, Maude, and tens of thousands of workers and retirees and their families. Unions are a community, dedicated to past, present, and future workers; to their companies, communities, and nation. My name is on those benefits checks. I must protect the rights of those who came before me, of my generation, and of those who will follow.

I also play a significant role in the broader labor movement. As a union leader and mother of two, I understand the child care challenges that working families face. Parents need to know that their children are safe and well cared for, so that they can give their best at work. They also need to be able to pay for this care. I felt compelled to work with a coalition of unions, child care advocates, and parents to lobby for funding of a facilitated child care enrollment program in New York State. Many working families earned just enough to disqualify them from receiving subsidies to offset the cost of child care. Others had difficulty completing and navigating the complicated application process. Still others were not even aware that financial help was available. The resulting program addressed all of these issues by providing subsidies according to increased income eligibility guidelines, establishing a facilitated enrollment program to assist with application completion and streamline the review and approval process, and developing a community outreach program to educate families about the subsidies.

This child care program is just one of the programs administered by the Workforce Development Institute (WDI), which is a statewide organization that manages programs beneficial to New York State's working families. As a WDI board member, I have witnessed the impact of its programs, which includes hard and soft skills training for incumbent workers, workforce intelligence gathering, research related to "green" jobs, support of apprentice programs, and small-business assistance. WDI has created a space where the world of work can be examined and nurtured, and where possibilities are explored in order to provide workers, companies, elected officials, and the labor movement a future of substantive work and a sustainable future.

In addition to supporting workers through the WDI, I represent labor by supporting the work of the Capital District Area Labor Federation (CDALF). In 2000, the national American Federation of Labor-Congress of Industrial Organizations (AFL-CIO) implemented the New Alliance, which created regional labor federations to increase worker mobilization and labor movement recognition in local areas. The New York State AFL-CIO was the first state Federation to implement the New Alliance program and my union president appointed me to serve on the board of the CDALF. As one of its founding members, I worked with other local labor leaders to break down the barriers between local unions and bring affiliates together as one movement: private sector, public sector, building trades, teachers and professors, retail food workers, healthcare workers, hotel and restaurant workers, painters, postal workers, plumbers, firefighters, truck drivers, police, bricklayers, state workers, federal workers, city and village workers. We built trust amongst affiliates, organized, and began identifying ourselves as The Labor Movement. We were empowered by our commonalities and inspired by our differences. As a movement, we are a whole that is much greater and stronger than our individual parts. The CDALF continues to expand its influence for the betterment of working families by forging alliances between affiliates and community partners, by raising the consciousness of elected officials, and broadening the labor movement's vision on and impact. This work has only just begun.

Like Maude, I am also a thought leader. I have benefited from mentors who have provided opportunities and guidance. I listen to others and learn. Labor leaders also listen to me. In that light, I stand up for a consciousness shift, away from individualism and toward a collective strategy. I know that collective action produces good contracts. I see the benefits every day when pension checks are sent to our retirees, healthcare claims are paid on behalf of workers and their families, college scholarships are awarded to union members or their children, or life insurance benefits are provided to beneficiaries. I experience a broken heart each time one of our workers is laid off, injured, or has to have their child hospitalized. I mourn every member who dies. I celebrate when one is promoted, when their child graduates from college, when I hear about a marriage, the birth of a child, and retirement with a decent pension. I think of John Donne: "No man is an island ... Every man is a piece of the continent ... any man's death diminishes me, because I am involved in mankind ...."

With this essay I speak out about individual unions and organized labor's mission and the opportunities and responsibilities to advocate for all workers, not just ourselves. We must protect our own and advocate for members' rights and working conditions. Each union must do outreach and organize. But this is not enough. Collectivism is as American as apple pie. I think of Benjamin Franklin's comment at the signing of the Declaration of Independence: "We must all hang together, or assuredly we shall all hang separately." union leadership must re-educate our members to appreciate our own history and promote collective responsibility for all workers, not just members. We understand that without strong and prosperous companies, there are no decent wages and benefits. A country whose economy tolerates Walmart and full-time employees needing food stamps and dependent on emergency room healthcare is rotting from within. I recommend that discussions of collectivism be brought into union meetings, and be included in our newsletters and, on our websites, so they become part of all political endorsement interviews.

Like many of today's politicians running election campaigns, labor has made a conscious effort to retreat to the middle, where the gray serves as cover. Where what one stands for, believes in, and represents can shift, a bit to the right or to the left, depending on the winds of change. At one time this strategy may have had some value, especially within a political climate that views workers as relevant and labor as an economic partner. But this is not our current climate.

Today, the middle is a dangerous place to be. Workers need solid footing. An understanding of the current economic and political environment as it relates to them, their families, and their communities. This understanding will not come from politicians or corporate America, but it can and should come from the labor movement. To provide solid footing and foster this understanding, labor needs to step out of the middle. Labor must stand squarely on the side of working families and their communities, and do so in a manner that gains workers' trust and promotes collectivism. This is not about the labor movement saving workers—it is about empowering workers to take collective action to save their fellow workers.

Unions must lead by example. Much like the experience of those hospital workers empowered to organize so many years ago, I implore labor leaders to put individual differences aside and work together towards common goals that benefit all workers. Work collectively to break down the barriers that isolate workers and foster recognition of our interdependence. Labor must recognize all workers as belonging before workers will commit to join.

# WORKING STORIES

# LEARNING GROWING SERVING

Susan F. Hains

I retired in 2015. This momentous decision awakened memories and created much introspection over the life I have lived, the choices I have made, and the paths I have chosen. And it is all surrounded by the women's movement: gains made, understanding granted, recognition of the problem, and my progression through it all; my understanding of who I was and am, my contributions toward the general good, and the influences of the greatest significance.

"A Woman's Nation Pushes Back from the Brink," the newest Shriver Report, nicely sums up the societal, economic, and business status of women today. While women have made great strides forward, many still find themselves tottering on the brink. Contributing factors such as pay inequality, gender bias, job discrimination, pregnancy discrimination, the glass ceiling, and pre-established gender roles have resulted in a general sense of economic insecurity and the loss of an untapped pool of workforce potential for our communities, employers, and nation, as women find themselves struggling to keep their heads above water.

When I think back to my adolescence, I do not remember ever feeling that I could not do or be anything I wanted. I was lucky enough to have parents who assumed I would continue my education in college and obtain a degree. My mom was a college-educated woman; she graduated early from high school and went right into Queens College as a sixteen-year-old. I don't think she ever questioned her life's path at the time because she was too busy being a "good girl" and searching for approval from her parents. She chose to marry and have children, and entered the teaching profession when family finances required. My dad was never able to achieve a formal education and, I think, was upset by the fact that he could not support his family on his paycheck alone. He was always adamant about his role as the family protector and "the boss" of the house (a role that brought us into conflict as I grew older!). It always seemed to be an issue my mom would try to work around, and I think it limited her professional growth. She was so smart and such a wonderful teacher that she could have been an administrator, a professor, or a teacher trainer. Lost opportunities and potential! I watched and listened but, at the time, only skimmed the surface of the implications of my dad's role. What did I care if he needed to see himself as the "head of the household?"

I, too, was searching for approval from others from an early age. "Be a good girl, Susan." I think girls were, and sadly, still are, raised to be the pleasers, the mediators, the givers. The problem, as I see it now, is that, though able to access a college education (a huge gift from my parents), I was really not "free" to achieve anything other than the expected. I went to a Catholic co-educational college preparatory high school, where I never broke the rules and never even laughed when others dared to. My choices seemed to me to be limited to college or the novitiate of the Sisters of Charity, which some of my classmates chose. I won a Regents Scholarship and the World History Medal for highest GPA, and was an A student, but not a thinking student!

I was living within the established societal bubble, as were many of my contemporaries. I had been conditioned by life to see "women's roles" as my only possibility. I was going to be a teacher, like my mother, or a nurse, like my aunt. I was going to get married and have a family. I was not going to go into business or be a mathematician or a scientist. The sad thing is that I never looked for a different possibility, because I was happy with my choices. I knew I was smart, and assumed I would be independent and capable of supporting myself—if I had to. The paradigm didn't shift for me until much later in adulthood. I never considered breaking the rules or stepping away from the norm. I was a good girl. Women today are still being constrained by this paradigm, though to a somewhat lesser degree. It has started to shift slowly within our society, but we have not yet arrived at complete change.

My college years welcomed the nascent women's movement, and I began to listen to Betty Friedan and Gloria Steinem and Bella Abzug. I was not, however, ready to burn my bra or move out of my comfort zone, having wrapped up my future in a pretty package. Graduation, teaching, maybe marriage, children. Looking back now, what would, or should, I have done differently, if anything? I walked in peace marches and in Kent State protests, I boycotted classes and went to rallies, but I never truly stuck my neck out or put my future on the line. I never dug beneath the surface of the platitudinous language I was using. I was a "good girl." But I was not a thinker or an activist or an organizer while in school. That would come later, as I began to see the world through others' eyes.

Teaching at that time was still a woman's career. As more men entered the field, changes began to take place. I was teaching in a small town, and was somewhat removed from the controversy pitting the New York State Teachers Association against the United Federation of Teachers. Our local association stayed connected to the National Education Association, but I remember Albert Shanker and Tom Hobart clashing, as their groups merged for the benefit of both sides. My mom, though, was in the thick of it: walking on picket lines in support of fair wages, longevity, and job stability, and debating with relatives and school board members ("those horses' asses!") about teaching and learning. I saw teachers making poverty wages while educating the children of the very people who didn't see the value in what their local schools were doing. I saw teachers whose jobs were dependent on serendipity and personal likes and dislikes. In those early years, I saw many women in the classroom. The very few men were mostly at the high-school level or in the administrative offices.

When I began working at a child care center, I saw working families of many races and ethnicities struggling to make ends meet while trying to place their kids in a safe learning environment. I saw moms and dads working day in and day out to create homes for their children. I understood then that families were not always comprised of married couples with kids, and that there was room to accommodate a great deal of diversity in the world. I saw firsthand what poverty does to growing minds and bodies, to communities, and to individual dreams and aspirations. I learned that sometimes it takes more than hard work to eke out a living, and that following the rules does not always result in multiple graces and a happy life. I was finally beginning to understand the "why" behind the demonstrations and the protests. This was reaffirmed on an almost daily basis during the years I spent at the Head Start Program. There I met strong men and women raising their children in less-than-ideal circumstances but giving them strength, resolve, and hope for the future. These parents held minimum-wage jobs (sometimes two or three) and worked long hours but still had a sense of common community. They taught me a lot about the unlocking of human potential made possible by proactive government programs, but even more importantly, they taught me about the loss of human potential when rules and regulations erect a wall that is impossible to climb.

The fact that women today have a more significant role in our society is due to the sacrifice and hard work of those women who endured the struggle to move it forward. Yet, there is still much to be done. After a late awakening, it was my turn to help make the workplace better for women. I have interacted with many women over the years, and have been able to put human faces to the statistics, and embrace their stories in solidarity with them. I have seen the determination and the struggle in women's faces; the despair and resolve; the successes and failures; and the human cost of bad public policy and misdirected resources. My purpose is to strengthen the resolve of all women; to offer them a pathway forward, regardless of their background or income; to better their work environment; to help them be more productive employees; and to use their talents and strengths to achieve a fairer workplace and work-life balance. In retirement, I keep that sense of purpose. It will continue to be relevant in all I do.

I was lucky that my life path took me out of the self-imposed boundaries I had unconsciously created and opened my eyes to other possibilities for women. I realized that my own nuclear two-parent family had moved from a societal norm to only one of many family structures. Career, single parenthood, self-support, and independence became part of the paradigm for younger women. But the workplace was, and is, slow to respond to changing societal mores. Flexible work schedules, pay equality, paid family and sick leave, healthcare, pregnancy accommodations, and access to quality child care could address some of the work-life stress in many women's lives and mitigate some of the issues limiting women's access to well-paying, stable jobs. Yet, little attention has been paid to institutionalizing these types of policies in order to foster a reasonable work-life balance.

The research has been done, statistics gathered, countless articles written. Coalitions have been formed and resources committed. Yet, women are still on the brink, in many instances living paycheck to paycheck due to circumstances beyond their control. Leaders in government and corporate America have been slow to respond to the crisis facing working women and working families across the United States. The human cost to individuals, families, communities, and businesses when women's job opportunities are limited by outdated workplace policies, non-equitable wages, and government's failure to mandate necessary social change has been studied again and again. Yet, as a case in point, after two years of advocacy work, the Women's Equality Agenda Coalition in New York State has yet to be passed by the legislature.

Today, working women often find themselves single-parenting with no child support, and a choice between a minimum-wage job and public assistance. They often live far from family but want to join the workforce to support themselves and their children. It is a sad fact that women represent nearly two-thirds of minimum-wage workers. Twenty-two percent of minimum-wage workers are women of color. A woman working full-time and year-round at the federal minimum wage of $7.25 per hour earns just $14,500—more than $4,000 below the poverty line for a family of three. In addition, women are typically paid only 77 cents for every dollar paid to their male counterparts. In other words, there is still a 23-cent wage gap. This gap is even wider for women of color: black women working full-time, year-round, make only 64 cents, and Hispanic women only 54 cents, for every dollar paid to their white, non-Hispanic male counterparts. Increasing the minimum wage to $10.10 per hour would boost annual earnings by $5,700, to $20,200, enough to pull a family of three out of poverty. More than 15 million women would get a raise, including more than one in five working mothers. A mother with two children working full-time at the minimum wage would earn just enough, instead of falling more than $4,000 below the poverty line.

The cost of accessible high-quality child care enters the conversation at this point. This family of three with an income of $20,200 is earning just above the poverty level. If the two children are three and four years old, the cost of high-quality licensed child care can run as high as $11,700 annually in New York State, which is unsustainable with the family's budget.

The women who have accessed WDI's Child Care Subsidy Facilitated Enrollment Program are real examples of the need to pay a wage that can support a family. These women are often faced with the difficult choice of paying for quality child care or paying for their food, rent, and/or utilities. They are often forced to choose between lower-quality child care and quitting their jobs to stay home with their children. This makes no sense! The cost of a publicly funded child care subsidy is less than the cost of public assistance in most cases. An increase in the minimum wage, paired with publicly funded child care subsidies, would be good for families, children, communities, and businesses. It is short-sighted to let current budget restrictions impact the future. The availability of quality child care dramatically impacts a woman's access to work, job development, and career advancement.

I hope that I have lived a good life and made a difference in the lives of the many children and adults whose paths I have directly or indirectly crossed. I no longer believe that being a "good girl" helped me achieve anything. I grew, personally and professionally, by speaking about things that were important to me; by working together with others to accomplish necessary changes in my community, school district, state, and country; by advancing my career as I advanced myself. My loud mouth and soft approach have helped me be a strong advocate. I found a way to achieve personal satisfaction in both my work and home-life. My children are good people who were never told to be "good." They just were. It is a matter of pride that their dad and I raised three ethical, moral adults with a solid foundation of tolerance, a strong sense of family, and a deep gratitude for all they have been given. They are stronger in their convictions than I was at their age, and far less reluctant to stick their necks out for their beliefs.

It is my hope that all working women today, regardless of background or income, will find their own path forward: one which allows them to strengthen their self-knowledge and resolve; which offers opportunities to better their work environment; and which allows them to use their talents to achieve a fairer and more productive workplace for all.

# WORKING STORIES

# TRUE NORTH

Greg Hart

I am the regional director of New York's Adirondack North Country for the Workforce Development Institute. It is my home, my mission, and my privilege. I was offered this job almost seven years ago by WDI Executive Director Ed Murphy. He wanted to have a person in the Northern region, where there had not been one before. It intrigued me that the job would focus on analyzing what challenges rural New York communities faced in this region, how those problems translated to the rest of the state, and what could be done to assist working families. This is what we do statewide: build strategic partnerships and leverage resources to devise and deliver effective programs. I was instructed to listen, learn, participate, and build relationships.

The Adirondack North Country is the largest region in the state. It consists of seven counties, from Lake Ontario and the Tug Hill through to the St. Lawrence River Valley, and down the Adirondack Coast of Lake Champlain through the Adirondack Park. There is no major population center, only two micropolitan cities, Watertown and Plattsburgh. My friend at St. Lawrence University, Ben Dixon, stated that the region is united in demography but divided by geography. Ben doesn't remember saying it; I credit him anyway.

What I took from this statement was, first, that we have a very large footprint. Travel time is a challenge, with hours separating people from jobs, access to healthcare, or groceries. Second, we have a sparse population. My colleague, Vivian Benton, likes to remind me that we must all know each other in the North Country (which I, of course, deny. I am sure there are a couple I haven't met). Third, demographics are not on our side. We have an out-migration of people, particularly young people. This means that we are losing population and our young people are leaving. Closely linked with that is the fact that we have more of an aging population than state and national averages. Finally, the North Country is united in demography, with a mostly Caucasian population. We do have some areas of diversity, one being the St. Regis Mohawk Tribe in Akwesasne, an area that spans the Canadian-U.S. border. Others are the university towns, with diverse faculty, staff, and students, and a large military base (Fort Drum) outside Watertown. Demographics present some interesting challenges to cooperation. It is the geography as much as anything that has hindered cooperation, a sense of regional identity, and the efforts to find some common solutions to common problems.

It is fair to say there is no critical shortage of conflict from the United Nations to the local school board. Internationally, nationally, statewide, and locally, positions are taken, jaws set, and heels firmly dug in. Gridlock, as a symptom, sets the stage for almost perpetual conflict. It seems that simply making the effort to speak to those with opposing views is betrayal. Conflict is not necessarily a bad thing. Without it, an entire industry of conflict resolution and diplomacy would be out of work. Indeed, democracy, in all its messiness, uses conflict as source material. It can lead to collaboration and to building different, and maybe more effective, partnerships. The key is to tone down the rhetoric, listen, and work to find where areas of agreement exist. It is, of course, much easier said than done. I will examine three efforts that I believe have been important in bridging that geographic divide: the North Country Symposium, the Common Ground Alliance, and the Regional Economic Development Councils.

First, a bit about me, and how I came to be involved in this work. I grew up in this region, on the Canadian border. It is a 45th parallel north, meaning it is equidistant from the equator and the North

Pole. I suppose I was raised straddling two extremes. Like many of the kids I went to school with, my father was a World War II veteran and a blue-collar worker at one of the local plants. He was an industrial electrician and a union steward. My grandfather and his brother worked there at the same plant. They were Canadians who came to work in the States. I was no stranger to grievances, strikes, and picket duty as a means to achieving justice in the workplace. I believe it instilled in me a sense of working for the common good by working together.

I left the state for a time, and eventually moved to Central New York, where I settled down to one of my careers (which lasted 25 years). I worked for a large multinational manufacturer with multiple business units as a machinist and a computer numeric controlled (CNC) machinist. I held numerous positions in production; in the union representing the bargaining unit; and in labor-management committees regarding productivity, work sourcing (insourcing, not outsourcing), and training. The key was to find what topics people could come together on. Quite often, it was difficult. When we set up a labor-management framework for sourcing component manufactured parts, the company looked at it as a way to shift production (and responsibility for that production) out of the plant. The position I took as chair was to bring high-value work with hours (meaning jobs) and investment into the shop. What the company and union agreed to was a method to justify a temporary or permanent outsourcing of a component if we could balance it with a component brought in. On the labor side, we also agreed to engage in a process to justify machine tool purchasing.

Now, this type of approach was not universally embraced (by the company or bargaining unit) and it took a great deal of communication to build some degree of mutual trust. I used the same approach in areas of job evaluation and training. There was interest on the part of the company to combine job codes to gain flexibility. I worked to gain pay upgrades and training for affected workers as fair exchange.

My wide variety of interests led me to pursue education. I earned an Associate's and then a Bachelor's in Business Administration, and finally a Master's Degree in Labor and Policy Studies, all while balancing a full-time (and overtime) regular job, union responsibilities, and my family, in addition to schoolwork. This seems crazy, but I did spread it over 10 years. What really drove me was a desire to balance what I knew in the "real" world with formal education and survival. I wanted to have that degree so that, in case something happened with my job, I would have a backup plan. The economy was shedding manufacturing jobs in droves, as companies sent jobs offshore. One company after another in Central New York followed that pattern. Mine finally followed suit, closing the production business units in 2003. We were told that we could work for free and still not be competitive with workers in Asia. The loss of these well-paying blue-collar jobs was devastating to the economy and to thousands of families.

I was called into a meeting one day at the local building-trade counterpart to my manufacturing union. I was asked to develop a residential heating, air conditioning, and ventilation program. The challenge was to build a program from scratch and make it compatible with the local union. The target audience was dislocated workers among those losing their jobs with real manufacturers. I am forever grateful for the confidence the international and the local leadership had in me to offer such an opportunity. It was quite a challenge, with a lab to build, equipment and tools to obtain, a curriculum (lesson plans and labs) to develop, and all the approvals and certificates to get. I was the lead instructor and program coordinator. We graduated four classes in an approved 16-week offering, where participants earned industry-recognized credentials. Unfortunately, we ran out of students and were unable to keep teaching the class. I went to work as the HVAC instructor at Boards of Cooperative Educational Services (BOCES), and eventually as the service manager at a local HVAC manufacturer.

I moved back to the North Country, and was offered this job in workforce development. This job engages and motivates me every day to better understand the opportunities and challenges facing rural New York, and this region in particular. I began to meet with people and participate, and support efforts to do just that. I supported our organization's mission by joining committees and sponsoring events, training, and studies in manufacturing, energy efficiency, economic development, biomass, healthcare, and community.

## North Country Symposium

The focus of the North Country Symposium has been understanding economic and environmental challenges to the North Country, as well as the relationship to education and community. It is one of the critical events that brings people together and points the way toward wider conversation and cooperation.

St. Lawrence County is the geographic center of the region, and a study in bewildering contrasts. This big county has natural resources, and five universities and colleges, but also some of the highest unemployment and poverty rates in the state. Industrial closures and the loss of private-sector jobs, along with population decline, have been trends. The Burt family, St. Lawrence University alumni, wanted to make an effort to address this. The Burt Symposium was made possible through a generous endowment by the Burt family, and St. Lawrence University has been hosting it since 2003. The event brings together people from academia, government, community, and environmental groups to explore a specific area.

Previous symposia have explored ways to build sustainable local economies and communities. They have been ahead of their time on some topics. For example, how the local foods movement and building value-added agriculture can provide great opportunity to rural counties. This is not revolutionary today, but was a new approach at the time. There are still those who do not place value in any agriculture other than big dairy and commodities. When it was first presented in a symposium, what was being done in Vermont was eye-opening. Many asked why we couldn't do it in Northern New York. The concept of creating sustainable growth (the keynote set by WDI's Ed Murphy) by utilizing retention strategies and developing a community foundation is a new idea. Furthermore, the challenges facing rural education, consolidation, and demography were hotly examined, and continue to be, up to the present.

What defines the work of the Symposium is the grassroots organizing that comes out of it. There have been working groups (Action Teams) that have developed from breakout sessions. These groups have a range of participants and are willing to keep the topics going throughout the year. For example, the work of the Energy Task Force, which I am on, has addressed local issues, from energy efficiency to alternative energy to waste reduction. There has been work done that helped feed into the North Country Energy conferences. Work by other work groups helped supply information and best practices to the North Country Strategic Plan when it needed to be written.

## The Adirondacks

I grew up in and around the Adirondacks, and witnessed an example of the economic divide firsthand. Communities that bordered the Adirondack Park had greater flexibility in land usage, and seemed to do better. Business and industry often had better options for development. Even as a youngster I could tell the difference, as some communities struggled and others didn't.

I know of one effort in the Adirondacks where a wide range of participants began a concerted effort over a number of years to try and build a model of collaboration. One big question since the creation of the Park in 1892 is how to balance the needs, concerns, and protections of the natural environment with the human-built environment. Where do people work and what kind of work do they do living in and around the Park? The conflict between the level of protection and development was a logical outcome, with people coming to the discussion with a wide range of experiences and perspectives on the issue. The chasm between use and protection has been wide and entrenched, with both sides looking to win.

We have very visible evidence in cities where companies abandoned their downtown facilities and left them boarded up and turning into crumbling remnants of factories and warehouses. It is a downward spiral of disinvestment and eroding tax base. What happens in rural communities when work disappears?

I remember going on a family car trip cross country when I was a child. We went through parts of the West where deserted towns were crumbling into the prairie. I thought then that the "ghost town" was a fascinating place. Today, I wonder about the lives of the people and what became of them.

What has become very interesting to me is the effort to find a path of compromise that enables people with divergent views to work together for the common good. What the Common Ground Alliance began eight years ago was an attempt to get people from across the Adirondacks under one big tent to begin the process. The different parties had battled in courts, hearings, in the press, and in public forums for many years. How has this process changed the approach to development, jobs, the economy, and the environment? How did these folks do it?

There are tourism folk, environmental groups, and economic developers in conflict over rails or trails. You get the picture. The Adirondack Park Agency Chair at the time, Ross Whaley, stated famously that "Adirondackers would rather fight than win." It did become very apparent that problems affecting the Adirondacks were serious challenges to the future of the area in both the natural and built environments. Acid rain insidiously lowered the pH of Adirondack lakes and increased mercury and other contaminants from coal-burning plants in the Midwest. Climate change is a real threat to Adirondack ecosystems, as well as to a winter-based recreation economy. A long list of invasive species poses a threat to the forests and lakes. Crumbling infrastructure and declining communities make the region less likely to attract visitors and new residents. Compounding this was the lack of broadband and other amenities. The world was bypassing the Adirondacks, and a real question was being posed: How much longer could this go on?

## Finding Common Ground

Three people got together for coffee in the early 2000s. One of them led an environmental group, the second was an elected town supervisor, and the third was executive director of a community action group. These folks regularly looked at problems from very different perspectives, but one of them put a paper on the table with three words written on it: Community, Economy, and Environment. This began a process concerning how to get people talking with each other on issues that were critical to all. In this case, the common denominator was the dire situation of the region. As mentioned, there were the threats to the environment (such as climate change, acid rain, and invasive species), the community (infrastructure, housing, transportation) and economy (broadband, main street decay, healthcare).

The three people brought more participants to the table and formed a public-private grassroots organization called the Common Ground Alliance. They authored a document entitled "A Blueprint for the Blue Line." They established collaboration between state and local governments, non-profit organizations, stakeholders, and residents of the Park, all participating as equals. Brian Houseal, Executive Director of the Adirondack Council at the time, said: "We work to recognize the common good of the communities, residents, and resources of the Adirondack Park, not to further specific organizational, institutional, or individual agendas." It was also agreed that all participants would be reminded to leave "Axes, Egos, Agendas, and Logos" at the door. The Blueprint was written by a core group of volunteers, and was the centerpiece of the first Common Ground meeting in Long Lake in July 2007. The 149 attendees discussed, debated, and revised the document, highlighting 12 major points. They included two additional items of property taxes and healthcare. In each point, a rationale was included on that particular challenge and the potential actions that could be taken.

Houseal said that establishing a framework to analyze problems and set some process to solve them was one aspect of the Common Ground Alliance. Another was to establish trust, and that was going to take time. Over the next few years, the group did some remarkable things to raise attention. Perhaps for the first time, the group was able to speak with a unified voice to the government in Albany and Washington. The Adirondack Association of Towns and Villages released an important work on what was happening to communities within the Blue Line, those lands protected by state constitution as "forever wild." "Conferences were held and action plans were devised to address climate change. Attention was given to the impact climate change would be to winter recreation-based tourism. An Adirondacks group went to Albany for a showing, set up for legislators and state agencies, of the Wild Center's climate film *A Matter of Degrees.* High-speed telecommunication build-out was acknowledged to be as important to rural communities as electrification or telephone was in decades past. The American Recovery and Reinvestment Act of 2009 got the ball rolling by releasing critical funding to begin the process in the Adirondacks.

What would be the next steps? If point by point in the "Blueprint" were worked on by dedicated volunteers, what was the overall goal? There was an opportunity for some strategic planning of what kind of Adirondacks people would like to live in. Stay tuned.

## Regional Councils

Economic, workforce, and community development have each existed in separate worlds in our region. Communities and counties were often in competition for scarce resources. Regional cooperation was limited or non-existent. If there was a success in one area, it was viewed as a zero-sum game. Part of this can be attributed to geography (again!). The region has areas that have worked to carve out a recognized "brand." The Adirondacks (High Peaks, Olympics); Watertown, as Drum Country for Fort Drum; the Thousand Islands, with the Seaway Valley and Plattsburgh (Adirondack Coast, Montreal's American Suburb). There were plenty of places that were left out, as some had the ability to apply for and administer grants, and others did not.

Previous efforts didn't help foster a North Country identity. North-south configuration seemed to build on some previous partnerships and made some sense. Plattsburgh was aligned, in some degree, with the Capital Region (with Interstate 87 Montreal to New York City) and an emphasis on technology. It was referred to as Tech Valley, Watertown (the other micropolitan city) was more aligned with Syracuse, following Interstate 81 in what is called the "Creative Core." The State didn't exactly help, as some agencies didn't follow the "footprint" on what each part of the region was. What counties were in what region and where do you apply for funding?

With his election, Governor Andrew Cuomo sought to change the structure of economic development in New York State. The opportunity for economic development funding and projects would rest with how well the region came together. Two co-chairs for each region were chosen, along with business, government, academia, and labor members appointed to the Council. The Regional Economic Development Council (REDC) area would be the east-west configuration and resemble (sort of) the Departments of Labor and Empire State Development footprints. A majority of the Adirondack Park would be in the North Country, with some parts in the Mohawk Valley and Capital regions.

The first step was for counties and communities to create a strategic plan. There were plans galore, from County Economic Development Strategy (CEDS) to tourism plans to sub-region plans, but nothing defining the entire region. The strategic plan process brought many people into the work that previously had not worked together or been offered a chance to engage. This includes me and the WDI, as I worked on the Workforce Strategy. We and other region-wide organizations, such as the Adirondack North Country Association (ANCA), brought experience in understanding what was happening on the ground. The groups and subgroups worked on their parts independently and *pro bono*. It was a remarkable project that came up with a uniquely North Country approach that positively addressed the opportunities and assets, without ignoring the barriers.

A statewide pot of funding was scooped together and made available to regions, with additional money going to those that linked development projects with the regional strategy. They won "Best Plan" designation. The applications (Consolidated Funding Applications) were reviewed and ranked, and the regional folks were able to add points to applications they felt reflected regional priorities. So, here is the interesting thing. Despite the real and perceived problems with this process, it worked on a number of levels. First of all, it brought a regional strategy to a scattered region (geography again?). People understood that the key to success or failure rested on forging new partnerships. Second, it democratized the process. I heard in the first year some grumbling from experienced economic developers that the REDC process was overly influenced by "well-meaning amateurs." If that was true, it was a good thing. It brought interesting, and perhaps non-traditional, projects forward for consideration from all corners of the region. Third, it became a framework for other community development and environmental funding. Through the CFA process, funding for the Opportunity Agenda and Cleaner, Greener Communities was awarded. Lastly, an atmosphere of competition in the region made good applications better and more aligned with the regional strategy. The regions were also in competition for "Best Plan" for those additional dollars.

## Conclusion

I have learned an incredible amount over the past seven years about this region and the people who call it home. I propose some of my closing comments apply to other rural communities across the state. First, regarding geography, it doesn't necessarily have to be something that divides. For example, there has been a great effort made by the Federal and State governments to close the digital divide. The access to high-speed, reliable broadband infrastructure has connected people, business, and needed services. It is as fundamentally important to rural communities as roads, electrification, and telephone. It shrinks the distances. WDI worked with our partners at Cornell Cooperative Extension to deliver, across rural counties in the state, a training program for women working in agriculture. They had access to high-quality training that was shared to remote locations. I have regular board meetings with organizations that are in Central New York and the Southern Tier. The technology is here and readily available.

Demography is not destiny. That phrase comes from a work on societal aging by Robert Friedland and Laura Summer. With regard to our rural Adirondacks North Country, I take the phrase to mean this: take assessment of the changes and commit to them, reverse, or change course. Certainly easier said than done, but not impossible. For example, we have held diversity summits over the last couple of years. Many in the Adirondacks have acknowledged that the region must be more welcoming to people of color and the LBGTQ community. Visitors, and how visitors want to experience our region, have changed as society has changed. People want a welcoming and safe place to explore, and (hopefully) to return to or tell their friends about. Embrace it.

Another issue, the retention and attraction of young people to our region, has its own challenge. Our universities and colleges bring a wonderfully diverse population of students (and faculty), but it is difficult to keep them without employment opportunities. I believe that the regional councils and the expanded approach to economic and community development are a good start to the integrated approach to sustainable communities. This past year, WDI funded work with the St. Regis Mohawk Tribe around Cultural Tourism. This effort is a way to showcase the cultural identity of our native craftspeople and artisans in a way that engages them actively with surrounding communities and visitors. This is obviously good for the Tribe, as a destination for visitors, but also for the region, to have such an important, enriching asset to share their culture and rich history with others, and it will be on their terms.

Finally, in searching for common ground, the examples I presented are action-based, stemming from serious threats. Problems are like conflict, coming in all shapes and sizes. Brian Houseal said that the Common Ground approach was a great example that could be replicated. I agree. It was difficult to lower the volume, and establish some trust and mutual respect, but it worked. A similarity between the Symposium, Common Ground, and the Regional Council is the grassroots approach. Groups coming out of the Symposium are citizen-based, and work on issues that come out of the yearly event. They take action and report ongoing activity. People have taken the structure and organized around it. The Common Ground

Alliance operates along the same lines, with people volunteering time and talent to push the solutions and policy that can change the demography. Lastly, the REDC came together, and people began to truly act more regionally.

I believe that this important discovery by a majority of Adirondack stakeholders has fueled closer and more coordinated efforts. In tourism, for example, a major initiative called the Adirondack Park Recreation Strategy was unveiled at a Local Government Day Conference that links the natural assets and the nearby community. I was walking out of that event with members of the Department of Environmental Conservation, and they were very encouraged by so many people talking about "our Park," and wanting to work more regionally. An Adirondack non-profit summit was held to highlight the economic impact of a number of those organizations in the Park. The Adirondacks are developing an economic development strategy, with clear, interrelated steps to get it done.

By no means have we become a strife-free zone, especially among committed and impassioned people. (There is still some sitting around campfires, though.) Organizations, government, and groups will dig their heels in when guiding principles and values dictate. In most cases, it is the tenor that has changed. This method of working together is certainly grassroots. That disclaimer is made at different meetings, and it welcomes in all stakeholders on all levels. People are engaging with state agencies more as partners, less as opponents. The level of trust and personal contact had to be established. This took time. It is important not to get too far ahead of the people. Some elected officials lost their positions as a result of their work with and on Common Ground Alliance projects. What the Alliance did that was critical was that it got people talking to decision-makers with one voice and reading from the same page.

# WE'VE GOT TO GET BACK TO THE GARDEN

Brian L. Houseal

My career began with a woman. It was summer, and I was 14 years old and deeply in love with a girl whose name I can't remember. I asked her out to the movies. My only problem was that I didn't have any money. So I asked my father if he could give me some. His response was, "I house, feed, and clothe you and your five brothers and sisters. If you want money to take your lady friend to the movies, go get a job." It was Friday afternoon after work hours, and when I asked my dad how to find a job, he suggested I walk up the street right away and speak with our neighbor, Fred Gabriel, a local contractor who built single-family housing subdivisions. I did. Fred said, "Sure. We'll pick you up at eight tomorrow morning. Bring your lunch and wear construction boots."

The next morning, Fred's pickup was in front of our house. I climbed in, and worked non-stop for the next eight hours on a housing subdivision: shoveling gravel into a basement, carrying shingles up a two-story ladder to a roofing crew, and spreading topsoil and seeding grass. I returned home aching and exhausted, took a shower, and fell asleep before dinner. I never did get to the movies with the girl.

At the end of that work-week, Friday afternoon, we gathered in Fred's garage for an ice-cold Rheingold beer, the first one I'd ever had, and probably the best one. Fred asked his work crew how the 'kid' had done, and they responded, "Pretty well, but he has to learn to pace himself; he makes the rest of us look bad, but we'll keep him." After more teasing and laughing, I was handed my first pay-check, $125. I couldn't believe I could earn that much money in one week. I was hooked.

For that summer, I worked on the landscape crew under the tutelage of two aging Italian immigrants, relatives of Fred's extended family business. They had come from the old country as stonema-sons to build the Pennsylvania Railroad. I never got their real names but learned to refer to them as *pisa, gumba,* or *compa.* They only spoke broken English that was so mixed with a heavy dose of Italian swear words as to be unintelligible to me. I watched them closely and learned by example as we built the many stone retaining walls needed in the hilly terrain.

Although both were over 70, they could move boulders weighing more than a ton, using levers and sledges. They would either laugh or swear at me if I tried to muscle a large stone, graphically demonstrat-ing what a hernia might do to my young sex life. I learned the art and craft of stone walls, and still love the intimacy of one rock inter-locking with others to form a structure that may endure centuries of snows and thaws, provide animal homes, and define human borders.

Throughout high school, I worked for the same construction company during summers, weekends, and vacations. I only had to call the night before and show up in the morning. The paychecks paid for part of my college expenses. When I turned 18, my father shook my hand, told me that I was a man, and on my own financially, because he and my mother had younger ones to support. Looking back now, years later, I realize that one of the greatest gifts my father gave me was the ability to ask for a job, and then do it well. And the best part of the job was that I learned every step in building houses from foundations to chimney's, including finish cabinet, reading architectural plans, landscaping, and dealing with people.

Armed with a Liberal Arts degree from Colgate University, and exposed to the cultural shifts in our society in the late 1960s and early '70s, catalyzed by Vietnam, hallucinogenic drugs, sexual revolution, and similar influences, I realized that my father's advice—to find a good corporate job and stay with it, as he had done for his entire career with AT&T—was not my desired career track. I was inspired by the lyrics of Crosby, Stills, Nash & Young: "We can change the world, rearrange the world ..." and "We've got to get back to the Garden...."

I enjoyed being in nature and building things, so I thought I might pursue a career in natural resource management. I hitchhiked to Syracuse and stopped at the State University of New York College of Environmental Science and Forestry (SUNY/ESF). I interviewed with the Dean of Admissions, Dr. Harry Payne. After listening to me carefully, Harry suggested that I was describing the landscape architecture profession, to which I responded, "Aren't they the ones who design gardens?" "Yes," Harry replied. "They are also the ones who design and build our national parks." That's what I wanted to do.

Harry walked me over to the Landscape Architecture Department, and Dean Brad Sear's office. In an engaging conversation, I learned that Brad had gained his experience with the Civilian Conservation Corps (CCC) during the Great Depression, designing and building Skyline Drive in the Shenandoah National Park. I was convinced that landscape architecture was the profession for me. Brad gave me a teaching assistantship that paid for my graduate degree because, as he put it, "You're the first grad student I've ever interviewed who knows which end of the hammer to hold and has actual construction experience." I had found a home, and it still serves me well.

An important aspect of my landscape architecture studies was an enhanced awareness of the incredible diversity and interrelationships of our planet, evolved through the interplay of geology, climate, soils, flora, fauna, and of course, human interactions with the natural world. Landscape architects call this a "sense of place": a culture's perception of a landscape and subsequent use of the natural resources, based on its prevalent beliefs and values. A people's knowledge of place is the yeast that, over time, produces unique and sustainable land uses, foods, building materials, architecture, art, literature, music, clothing, and the many other items of cultural diversity. The land shapes culture and culture shapes the land.

The best lesson of my graduate work was to discover my avocation. It can be summed up in three statements: the whole world a garden, every place with a garden, every garden with a gardener.

The whole world a garden. The bountiful garden concept is described in the Old Testament and other religions' sacred scriptures. The Garden of Eden is an apt metaphor, whether or not we believe in that place, where daily sustenance was easily gathered; or the Adam and Eve tale about the loss of innocence, parental authority, and punishment; or the true story about a talking snake and apples that make you wiser.

We now know that the degradation of the earth's natural systems is accelerating, and it is at our peril that we ignore the signals. So I set this first unattainable goal for myself: to restore the earth's ecosystems and natural processes. We've got to get back to the Garden.

Every place with a garden. Natural scientists have identified the earth's major biogeographical provinces, terrestrial and marine ecoregions, ecosystems, natural communities, and plant and animal species, albeit with many species still unknown. Within each of these classifications, we should be setting aside enough landscape or seascape to preserve a full array of all living species and their habitat for generations to come. Today we are failing as stewards of nature, and are facing the greatest and most rapid extinction of species since dinosaurs roamed the earth. Only this time, we the people are causing it by destruction of natural habitats; over-exploitation of commercially viable plants, animals, and fish; polluting the atmosphere; and raising the planet's temperature beyond survivable limits for many species. We need to set aside large core natural areas, create corridors among those areas, and design permeable landscapes for the free-flow of species, unimpeded by built structures such as cities, hydroelectric dams, or other barriers.

Every garden with its gardeners. In order to succeed in reversing the degradation and loss of habitat and the species they contain, we need a new generation of scientists, planners, designers, and natural resource managers who have both a global understanding of the threats our current civilization face, and the creative, entrepreneurial, and leadership skills to change societal behavior. Even though it may sound anthropocentric, we need to become "planetary managers" and begin a new era of restoration, and set in place corrective societal behaviors so we might live in harmony with the multitude of species with which we share this special place. Training the next generation to take over the helm of "Spaceship Earth" (Buckminster Fuller's term) is paramount in my work.

While writing the final chapters of my graduate thesis on the Adirondack Park, I got lucky beyond my expectations. My advisor, George Earle, explained to me that he had just returned from Chile's Patagonia region, and their National Forest Corporation (CONAF) needed a landscape architect to design and build a new national park that "looked like Yosemite, only a hundred years ago." He asked whether I knew of anyone who might be interested in going there to work. "Yes," I replied, "and please don't tell anyone else." The luckiest part was that the most important woman in my life, my wife, Katherine, said, "Yes, let's go on this adventure." I had landed an international job in my desired profession to go to a wilderness I could only imagine.

In 1976, Katherine and I were accepted by the U.S. Peace Corps, specifically for positions in Chile's Torres del Paine National Park, a spectacular and remote place at the southern tip of South America. Our work was to assist CONAF in converting an extensive 250,000-acre sheep ranch to a national park and building infrastructure for tourism. It was indeed like Yosemite over a hundred years ago, after sheep had overrun that valley. It took a major effort by the Chilean government to restore the heavily degraded land and create an enduring national park that has become a world-class destination today.

Our first impression of Torres del Paine was that it was a scene from a J. R. R. Tolkien novel, with impassable windswept mountains, stunted ancient trees, and foreboding ice caps and glaciers. From our doorstep, we could see real wilderness, where no human being had set foot.

Remoteness is a relative term in today's 2015 society (which includes the Internet), so I will describe it. Katherine and I lived in a park guard outpost on Lago Grey. It was a 25-mile horseback ride from the park's administrative center at Lago Toro, and took another six hours in a four-wheel-drive vehicle to get to Puerto Natales, the nearest town where we could buy supplies. To the west, our nearest neighbor was Pochongo, a hermit who lived in a sheepherder line shack about 15 miles away, at Lago Zapata, which drained directly from the overhanging continental ice-sheet. We suffered from bouts of loneliness, as a month would pass without seeing anyone or hearing news from the outside world.

We were also excited by working in a place so sublimely spectacular that it could take your breath away in the alpine-glow of a mountain sunset. For those who have never experienced self-reliance in the wilderness, trust me, it's very humbling, and you don't want to screw up, because someone may die.

If I had been a fledgling landscape architect for the U.S. National Park Service (USNPS), it would have been years before I would be given the task of designing and building a national park, but here I was, at 26 years old, with that awesome opportunity. My CONAF counterparts, the park director and construction foreman, were also recent university graduates. We would spend evenings discussing priority construction project designs, available materials, and crew schedules. Our designs were built into trails, roads, bridges, visitor interpretive centers, and lodgings which are still in place today.

One interesting learning experience was when the three of us decided to widen a particularly dangerous blind curve on the main road along the Pehoé Lake shore, where a head-on traffic accident had occurred. There was a 40-foot-high cliff of shale that had formed a "nose," which we intended to blast to improve the sight distance. None of us had ever used dynamite, but we studied the techniques in our engineering manuals and convinced ourselves that we could do it. In the field, we surveyed the line and had the crews manually drill the postholes to set the charges. When the big day arrived, we cautiously placed the dynamite, and wired it to the plunger at a safe distance. The explosion was loud, and the rock face crumbled exactly as we had planned. But, within seconds, there was a second crash from a half mile away, at the island's tourist hotel across Pehoé Lake. We hadn't calculated the sound wave, and blew out two stories of ten-foot-high plate glass windows. The next morning, a terse telegram appeared from the regional chief: "NO MAS DINAMITA!"

After a year in the park, we realized that there was no manual in Spanish for the design and construction of national parks, so we wrote one. Several editions were published by the Food and Agricultural Organization of the United Nations (FAO) over the coming years. Again, I was lucky insofar as there was no other reference material available in Latin America, and my name became associated with building national parks and protected areas at a time when those developing countries wanted the economic development that nature tourism could bring. I've been working my way north from Patagonia ever since.

We returned from Patagonia to the U.S. with a new son, Ian, born in Punta Arenas, within sight of the Strait of Magellan. As a young out-of-work father, I knocked on many doors, and was rewarded by a short-term consultancy with the United Nations Man and the Biosphere Programme to advise the Honduran government on the creation of the Rio Plátano Biosphere Reserve on the Caribbean Coast.

As the pilot and I flew from the Honduran capital of Tegucigalpa over the Continental Divide, the landscape changed from cattle pastures and patches of coffee plantations to lush tropical rainforest cover. After circling low to chase the grazing cattle off the grass strip, we landed near the beach, and I walked the five miles into the village of Barra Plátano alone. There I met our team of five from the Honduran Ministry of Natural Resources. My official charge was to undertake an assessment of the natural resources of the 500,000-acre Río Plátano watershed, recommend boundaries for a proposed Biosphere Reserve, and estimate a three-year budget.

A day later, we loaded our gear on tuc-tucs and headed upriver for a week-long expedition into the uncharted territory of the upper Río Plátano. It was an intriguing trip, due to rumors of a fabled lost "White City" built by ancient people who left curious pictographs carved into large boulders along the river course, and the archeological remnants of elaborate tools and grinding stones found in the area. After we had passed upriver rapids beyond the last native settlement, we entered old-growth tropical rainforest, with magnificently tall trees, abundant vines, orchids, and the hidden sounds of birds, monkeys, and other unseen animals. So this was the Garden, I told myself. This is the way the world once was.

Our expedition had been traveling along the river for a few days when I decided to travel into the forest interior to get a better sense of it, and asked for a guide to accompany me. We would reunite with the group several miles further upriver at day's end.

The change from the open sunlit river to the jungle darkness was immediate. My field of vision reduced from hundreds of yards to only several feet in front of me. A green and confusing wall of vines, leaves, tree trunks, and branches obstructed our way. Beside me, a barefoot native guide in gym shorts and a tee shirt, armed with a machete, pointed in the direction we should go. I didn't speak his dialect and he didn't speak Spanish. I followed him along a game trail, and inhaled the dank richness unique to tropical rainforests, and began to question leaving my colleagues on the river.

About an hour into our hike, my guide suddenly laid the flat side of his machete across my chest, stopping me. I looked at him, he looked at me and smiled, and then he looked to a place about a foot in front of my face. Then I saw it. An 18-inch-long emerald-green eyelash viper was directly in front of my head, with jaws wide and fangs bared, ready to strike, and I had missed it. The snake blended in perfectly with the thin vines and leaves where its prehensile tail was attached. If bitten in the face or neck, I would die. I spent the remainder of our hike hallucinating on every leaf, vine, and root. We rejoined our team before sunset. I ate a hearty meal and dropped into an exhausted sleep. I had learned about the Garden, snakes, and wisdom.

Returning from Honduras, I found work in beautiful Saratoga Springs, New York, with the LA Partnership, where I completed the required two-year apprenticeship and passed the New York State Landscape Architecture licensing exam. Soon afterward, international work called again, when Dr. Craig MacParland, of the Tropical Research Center, asked if I would be interested in being a consultant to Panama's fledgling national parks system, as a component of the Panama Canal Treaty. Katherine was six months pregnant with our second son, Patrick, and when we learned that a live-in maid would be an affordable option, we left for another adventure.

As with many other Latin American countries of that period, Panama was governed by a military dictator, General Omar Torrijos, and referred to as a "Banana Republic." I was exposed to the reason as soon as I went to Panama City's Customs building with a borrowed pickup truck to retrieve the household gear we had shipped ahead. After I presented my papers, the customs official looked across the warehouse and pointed out the pallet with our belongings, then put on a long face. "Ah," he sighed. "It will probably take a week to inspect it all." "A week!" I exclaimed. "My papers are in order, I've got a truck outside, and my wife and children need those things today." Then I understood. "Perhaps I've missed one of the fees that are necessary?" I asked politely. "Would $20 cover it?" His eyes brightened, and he replied, "As our General Torrijos has said, 'He who gives love receives love.' Over his shoulder, he called to his workers, "Pepe, José! Put that pallet on his truck." "Welcome to Panama," I quietly said to myself. Corruption was an acceptable way of life in certain sectors of their society, and we would see it many times during our six years in the country.

I was hired by the Panamanian Institute of Natural Resources (INRBNARE) as consultant to the newly created National Park Service and counterpart to the director. The project was funded by the U.S. Agency for International Development (USAID) to ensure that the watershed of the Panama Canal was protected for the continued operations of interoceanic shipping. Soon after arriving in my new post, it became clear that I worked for Panama, and there was considerable animosity among the "Zonians." These were U.S. citizens who were born and raised in the Panama Canal Zone, who believed that I had betrayed the cause of retaining the Canal for America.

One of my new national park team's first tasks was to take over the ex-Canal Zone lands and establish the "Soberania" (i.e., Sovereignty) National Park. Resented by the Zonians, and with poor, landless Panamanians pressing against the tropical rainforest boundaries and becoming agricultural squatters, the park director, Raoul Fletcher, and I had our hands full.

While patrolling one afternoon, we discovered a newly opened jeep road into the park's tropical forest and followed it to where we came upon a Panamanian military platoon and a large bulldozer. Incensed, Raoul hopped from our jeep and confronted the lieutenant, informed him that they were inside the national park, and emphatically ordered him to stop the illegal road construction. Eight nearby privates stopped to watch the exchange. The lieutenant told us he had orders to build the road, but Fletcher didn't back down, and shouted that they had to leave immediately. The lieutenant's next move was decisive. "Listos! Apunten!" (Ready! Aim!). The eight men immediately unslung their rifles, cocked, and aimed at Raoul and me. Then I spoke for the first time in this encounter. "Lieutenant, there has apparently been a misunderstanding. Forgive us, please. We'll be leaving now." I gave Raoul one of those sidelong looks that implies "Don't open your mouth again!" The lieutenant had saved face in front of his men and ordered them to stand down. Raoul and I walked slowly back to our vehicle, got in, and drove away. It would not be the first or last time that the Panamanian military ignored the country's national park law to extract precious timber or other resources when they found it convenient.

It was an honor to work with Panama's fledgling park service to establish many new protected areas, especially the ones declared as UNESCO Biosphere Reserves due to their natural and cultural resources. Panama has not only conserved an incredible array of biological diversity in these reserves, but it has also respectfully protected the territories of rainforest, where indigenous groups have lived for millennia.

After four years with INRBNARE, I was offered a new consultant contract for two years with the Kuna people. Their territory extends along the northeastern slope of Panama's Continental Divide to the coastal Caribbean Islands; basically from outside the port city of Colón to the Colombian border. The Kuna have a strong oral tradition, and can recount events such as the Great Flood, the day Columbus first landed on their shores, and their fight for independence from Spanish invaders, whose influences, in the form of Panamanian culture, they still resist today.

The Kuna opened my eyes to an indigenous view of the world as their garden, with them as the gardeners. They believe Kuna people were born from Mother Earth and are intimately linked to all living plants, animals, and the spirits (called *ponikana*) which inhabit the land and water. To them, rain is the Great Spirit making love to Mother Earth. The tropical rainforest and Caribbean Sea are the sources of their economic life. A tribal elder once asked me the prices of my house, car, food, medicine, and other commodities, then proceeded to educate me how his thatched home, sailboat, food, pharmaceuticals, etc. were all free because they came from the land, water, sky, and sun. "I am a rich man," he declared. Indeed, he was.

My work with the Kuna was to establish a defense boundary between their tribal lands and the oncoming slash-and-burn agriculture and cattle ranching from the Panamanian side of the mountains. Our team of Kuna cartographers and volunteers from their island communities cut a swath along their border, posted, and patrolled it against illegal incursions. The only impediment was when a peasant farmer would show us his permit, signed by a Panamanian colonel, indicating he had ownership to the land he cleared, even though it was on Kuna territory. My Kuna counterparts contested such claims with Panama's Ministry of Justice but gained little satisfaction due, once again, to corrupt military. General Manuel Noriega had become the dictator, and drug-running, money laundering, arms trafficking, selling tropical hardwoods, and other illicit activities had become his and his cronies' businesses.

During the same time, stopping tropical deforestation in Central America was in vogue with U.S. conservationists, and it was easy to communicate the Kuna's cause to the media. However, it did have its consequences. One evening, as I drove home from the Kuna field station on the mountainous Continental Divide, two Panamanian soldiers stopped my vehicle when I reached the Pan-American Highway. They asked for my papers, as one shined a flashlight in my eyes and the other pointed his rifle at me. I had international diplomatic immunity, so I was more angry than afraid but kept silent as they slowly reviewed my documents. Finally, they handed them back, and warned me, "You need to be careful out here at night; it can be dangerous."

A military source, who was a friend, informed me a few days later that Noriega wondered who had gotten those "little Kuna people" into *The New York Times*, and that I was being watched by the D-2 Military Intelligence Unit. The same day, Katherine and I had a conversation about leaving Panama as soon as possible. The U.S. invaded a year and a half later in 1989 to remove Noriega.

In my final months in Panama, I consulted to the Nature Conservancy's International Program to create the successful non-profit National Association for the Conservation of Nature (ANCON), which played a vital role in protecting the national parks after USAID funding terminated. Our pending departure from Panama corresponded with the Conservancy's need to hire a protected areas expert in their Washington, D.C., office, and I was asked to come for an interview.

As I reviewed the Conservancy information on the American Airlines flight north, the fellow across the aisle asked if I worked for them. "No, but I'm headed for an interview," I replied. We fell into an easy conversation about what remaining natural areas needed to be saved in Latin America and the Caribbean. I removed the airlines map and drew circles around many of the large areas, from Patagonia to Mexico, as he queried me about their conservation values. As we deplaned, he introduced himself as David Younkman, a member of the Conservancy Latin American team. Dave and I would soon design the Parks in Peril program, in large measure based on that airplane map and a good conversation. He is still a good friend.

In my new position as Director for International Stewardship at the Conservancy, a very astute board member, Cliff Messinger, asked me if I knew what it would take to "lifeboat" threatened parks and reserves in Latin America . "No," I quipped, "but if you can find me some walking-around money and give me six months, I'll have a response." "You're on," he replied. Within three months, our small team had logged tens of thousands of airline miles meeting with directors of national park services throughout the Latin American and Caribbean regions, reviewed maps and scientific reports, and designed a strategy to secure U.S. congressional appropriations. Initially, we identified 200 places, and named the program Parks in Peril. Our formula was simple: establish on-site protection, integrate the protected areas into the economic and cultural lives of local communities, and create long-term funding mechanisms to sustain local management.

I appreciated the opportunity to have led the design and manage the Parks in Peril program, along with many Conservancy colleagues and partner organizations, for its first ten years, from 1990 to 2000. The program lasted for 17 years, operating in 45 protected areas, totaling 44.8 million acres in 18 countries, with 200 partner organizations, with a direct investment of $105 million. Finally, many places were set aside as gardens, and those gardens had gardeners.

September 11, 2001, changed our world with the attacks on the World Trade Towers in New York City, and the Pentagon in Washington, D.C. September 11 is also my birthday, and having 3,000 people die the same day was profoundly saddening for me, and is now an annual day of reflection to contemplate my purpose in life. It is gratifying to have had the opportunity to live in some of the most beautiful places in our hemisphere, working to conserve our natural world, rather than for destructive forces of life.

Post–9/11, it was immediately apparent that U.S. interests in the world had shifted away from conservation in Latin America to a war footing in Afghanistan and the Middle East in general. It was time for me, professionally and personally, to transition away from international conservation and return to a U.S. domestic position. In 2002, I became the executive director of the Adirondack Council, and moved to the 6.1 million-acre park in northern New York.

The Adirondack Park has been contested terrain for over 150

years, since the establishment of the "Forever Wild" Forest Preserve, when large tracts of land were permanently protected by the New York State Constitution. In 1974, the creation of the Adirondack Park Agency (APA) further exacerbated the conflicts between development interests of local communities and environmental organizations pushing for more preservation and stricter land-use regulations. The Adirondack Council was created at the same time to advocate for the fledgling APA, and became a target of community animosity. The situation had not changed significantly over the intervening years as I took over my new position.

In 2005, Lani Ulrich, then-director of a non-profit economic development organization, asked J.R. Risley, supervisor of the Town of Inlet, and me to meet. It was an attempt to overcome decades of conflict in the Adirondacks. When I asked Lani what the agenda was, she produced one question: "Can we find solutions that benefit Adirondack communities, their economies, and the environment?" That question has given rise to the Common Ground Alliance, a group of over 150 Adirondack citizens dedicated to finding those solutions and speaking to our legislators in Albany with one voice to accomplish positive changes to our region. I am proud to have been a co-founder of a regional movement which has changed the tenor of the debate from conflict to compromise, and from viewing the Forest Preserve as an imposition to seeing it as an opportunity. We have accomplished this effort at a time when our national political debates are more polarized and unable to address major environmental challenges, social and economic inequality, and the loss of our democratic leadership around the world.

I will leave you with a metaphor about what may lie ahead by looking backwards. During the Medieval Ages, European people spent hundreds of years and all the excess capital in their societies to build Gothic cathedrals, the architectural flowers of the time. Why? Because they believed in God, heaven, and hell, and that they would get to heaven if they bought indulgences. Today, our architectural wonders are multinational corporate headquarters. Why? Because we believe in the dollar, free markets, global capitalism, and that unrestrained profit is good. Both of these examples demonstrate how societal values drive outcomes.

So, what values must we have as societies so that the next cathedrals are green and blue, and celebrate all the life we share in this garden we call Earth? A Dene shaman in Canada had an answer: "Water, and every living thing that depends upon it, is sacred. Heal the waters, and all else will improve too." We are getting back to the Garden and beginning a new Age of Restoration.

# WORKING STORIES

# THE PATH UNPLANNED

Lois Johnson

I was always a little out of step in my working-class Upstate New York town. As the eldest daughter in a gaggle of eight kids growing up during the 1960s and '70s, my liberal, anti-war, pro-civil rights, pro-union Irish-Catholic mother from Berkeley, California, pretty much guaranteed that. She was passionate about current events of that era—Vietnam War, Civil Rights, poverty, Watergate—and expected that you could discuss them knowledgeably around the dinner table and out in the world. I was often in hot water after expressing some of those dinner-table opinions at my small Catholic school. Apparently unaware of my mother's goal of raising opinion-ated rabble-rousers, Sister Alicia Marie sent a note home during the sixth grade, complaining of my negativity, after I stated publicly that I opposed the Vietnam War.

Being a member of this family also meant that you needed to get involved; to do work that benefited humanity in some way and made a difference in the world. In my imagined future, I would go to law school, and then work in some area of social justice. I took a differ-ent, unplanned path, however; one that ultimately birthed a passion for the ways we humans work, earn our living, and express our deep-est talents in the world. The places my life took me shaped a vision of a world where everyone, regardless of background, ethnicity, or socioeconomic status, has access to work that pays a living wage; where education and training provide each of us with the knowledge, skills, and foundational learning blocks to continuously learn and adapt in a rapidly changing workplace.

I didn't arrive there immediately or easily. Along with my strong opinions and deeply held beliefs, there wasn't much grounding me in how to actually implement that passion and vision in tangible ways, either in my life and out in the world. A big worldview, combined with a lack of practical skills for how to actually accomplish something, did not make for a successful life plan.

This meant that I wasn't ready for college, and I left after a disastrous year. I had a child not too long after that, and found myself a young single mother, with little education and few identifiable skills, not unlike far too many young people today.

Fortunately, I also never let what I didn't know stand in my way for very long. A natural curiosity and doggedness helped me learn what I needed in order to navigate through a much more circuitous path than the one in the original vision of my life. I needed skills and tools and methods, as well as knowledge, to express that deep longing to make a difference in the world. I needed recognition of the skills I already possessed, with a clear, attainable path for how to develop those that were missing.

Our earning potential and ultimate socioeconomic place in the world is largely determined by the work we do and the salary we can earn. Equally important, it also resolves whether or not the world gets to benefit from our talents and skills. Too many of us never show up on an employer's radar if we don't fit the traditional model for hiring qualified people. An invisible workforce often lives at the fringes, possessed of immeasurable potential, talent, skills, and energy, and yet, never making it past the Human Resources screening process.

As a young woman with no degree, and minimal experience, I certainly didn't look very promising on paper. In my limited understanding of the workplace and my own worth there, all I really qualified for where I could make enough money to support my child was restaurant work, waiting tables. It meant working nights, when the tips were better but child care was more of a challenge. I learned so many important skills in restaurants, though: how to motivate others, how to organize my time, how to multitask; plus, of course, customer service and communication. All of these are critical workplace skills and ones highly valued by employers.

Mostly though, I was just a smart young woman with tons of raw, unpolished energy, but still largely invisible to potential employers in other fields. There are far too many young people out there like that today, as well as many adults already in the workforce.

I saw this quagmire clearly. I knew I needed a different starting place; an entry-level job that would help me expand my skills, work my way up the career ladder, and build a résumé with increasingly responsible positions. Having a child so young taught me the value of just doing the next possible thing, breaking down what seems to be an insurmountable mountain to climb one step at a time, always moving forward.

I took a rather large pay cut to accept an entry-level human services position. I learned everything I could on the job. I took on extra responsibilities, read books and research papers in my field, and made it clear to my employers that I was willing to work hard and that I was hungry for more. I was promoted several times, took lateral moves to similar positions in different organizations, and eventually worked my way up to founding and directing my own not-for-profit workforce organization, and then scaling further to work on national workforce strategies and policy.

Like many working adults, I returned to college and completed a degree while working full-time. I truly enjoyed the intellectual experience, but at that stage, with a child and responsibilities, mostly returned to earn the credential. The degree would allow me far greater latitude in my work and open many more opportunities. Incidentally, but not coincidentally, I was now an excellent student, because of the skills I had absorbed and incorporated through work.

The truth is that, as a "consumer" of higher education, I was in many ways the norm, not the exception. College has been promoted as an important rite of passage for young people, as well as the ticket to the American dream of a successful career. The residential four-year-college experience, however, is inaccessible for many today, with its four-year requirement of money and time. In fact, less than a third of all undergraduates are "traditional" college students: that is, full-time, standard college age, and enrolled in a four-year public or private college. Many more commute, are enrolled in community colleges, work while taking classes, and attend only part-time, as finances and time allow.

My sister graduated from high school and attended a small liberal arts college, graduating successfully after four years. She is the model of what we think of as a traditional college student, and around which many institutions base their educational model. I, however, as a young, single parent, working while taking classes, first at the community college, then at a four-year university, stopping when I ran out of money and starting again when I could, was obviously not. It took me 10 years to complete my degree, which is, again, not uncommon. Based on the data, I, and the many others like me, are the norm, yet the vast majority of post-secondary educational programs are not designed with us in mind.

On the hiring side of the equation, more than half of employers are unable to fill positions in their companies. They complain that many candidates, including many college-educated young people, lack the fundamental skills necessary in a contemporary workplace. The skill sets needed in the workforce tripled between 2009 and 2012. Our current education and workforce development systems were not designed with this rate of technological and information change in mind. We are often unable to prepare workers for the continuous, career-long learning now required. Referred to as the "Learning-to-Learn skills," the ability to continuously receive and absorb new information and knowledge is critical for today's workers to stay competitive.

This need to always learn new things was a lot more challenging in my earlier years. I went to the library, sought out someone who could teach me, or just tinkered with it until it worked. I discovered the amazing resource of trained reference librarians. Today, if you want to learn how to start a business, or develop cash projections, or create an app, you can read about it on the Internet, watch a YouTube video, or take a free MOOC (Massive Open Online Course) from Stanford or MIT. If your math skills are weak, you can go online to the Khan Academy's numerous and excellent programs. There is a world of knowledge and learning media for today's workforce to choose from. This is not, nor should it be, solely the domain of the educated and the elite. Providing each of us with the access to learning in an accessible, flexible way; on our own schedule; from home if we want it, can provide the keys to the kingdom to all.

It is sometimes seen as anti-education to talk about workplace skills as a critical and much-needed outcome of our education system. Sometimes this makes for tricky conversations with family members (including my now-grown son) who are educators. As the country searches for ways to improve outcomes for our young people and current workforce, teachers and public schools justifiably feel under siege and unfairly blamed for factors out of their control, including massive changes in our economy and industry. Yet, some educators do reject the notion that schools should also prepare students for work, fearing that students will be "tracked" into low-expectation "vocational" programs, an antiquated term that carries a huge historical weight for many working-class people and students of color.

Yet, there are a lot of jobs, more than half, in New York State right now that require more than a high school diploma but less than a four-year college degree, referred to as "middle skills." Too few of our state's workers have the education and/or training to qualify for these positions. Many of these jobs pay higher wages and allow workers to learn new skills, earn additional credentials, and earn degrees as they progress on the job, much as my own self-designed career and education path proceeded. This is referred to as "stacking credentials," and also reflects the reality of today's workplace, where technology changes require continuous learning and skill development. Those of us who worked while studying, and incrementally accumulated skills and credentials and degrees, know that this has always been an option: it is now time to better articulate, and simplify, the path for those trying to navigate toward a successful career.

I've now worked in the field of workforce development for

many years and have approached the issues from multiple perspectives: helping disadvantaged women and youth successfully enter or re-enter the workforce, to raising the quality of state and local government-funded workforce programs, and supporting business and industry in successful hiring practices. This work has always been informed by the notion that we need to do something now. Long-term systemic change is ideal, but in the meantime, large numbers of young people are leaving our high schools and colleges unprepared for further education or a career, and many adults are finding a deep mismatch between the expectations of today's workplace and the skills which had previously kept them employed. The problems are even more acute among African-American and Hispanic youth, who are being left behind in truly unconscionable numbers.

Something needs to be done. We clearly need a new value proposition to address these issues.

We need a game changer.

Like me, many people must work while learning, so they need a combination of career and educational opportunities that allow them to develop these skills on the job or through a myriad of self-learning options. Innovators in the field of higher education and hiring are seeking ways to measure underlying cognitive skills. "Learning-to-Learn" skills allow us to rapidly attain new skills in a rapidly changing technological world. Many of us possess skills, having self-taught or learned them on the job, and we're finding ways to measure and credential them so that those skills can be demonstrated to employers.

These cognitive skills assessments do a far better job predicting on-the-job performance than education and experience. They are also an excellent way to provide a snapshot of where skills are lacking, allowing for more customized education and training that address what you actually need to learn.

This is revolutionary—a way to illuminate our invisible workforce and shine a spotlight on young people and older workers alike who possess real, substantive skills that any smart employer would be happy to get. The method they used to achieve those skills, whether from classroom learning, MOOCs, or on the job, should be immaterial. What they know and how they can demonstrate that mastery is the heart of the matter. Ultimately what is most important to employers is whether you have the skills to do the job.

I was fortunate to be both desperate and resourceful as a young woman. This led me to find the tools and mentors I needed to forge my own career ladder. While I never underestimate the privilege that my mother bestowed on me with her insistence on thinking and acting toward a better world, I also know how difficult it is to pull yourself out of poverty and create a life full of opportunity and possibilities for yourself and your children.

Finding new ways for people to learn and achieve credentials and degrees, and for employers to identify new pools of highly qualified candidates, has the potential to blast open the hidden doors for the far too many who have been barred from successful participation in both education and the workforce. This is a game changer.

I am my mother's daughter. She passed along her vision of fairness and justice. Life has enriched that big worldview in me with practical knowledge of how to make change in the world. Most of what I bring to my work these days is deeply informed by those earlier experiences.

Sometimes, and probably more often than not, the path we didn't expect to take in life takes us exactly where we're supposed to be.

# WORKING STORIES

# BLUEPRINT

Richard Lipsitz

I have been an activist since the mid-1960s. I remember reading, and being inspired by, biographies written for young people called Landmark Books. I probably read 50 of those books. Often, they were abridged versions of famous biographies, and some were written specifically for a teenage audience. During that time, I was acutely aware of the civil rights struggles against Jim Crow in the Deep South. One of my earliest teachers was a Freedom Rider, and his experiences affected me greatly. Having grown up in Buffalo, which was, and still is, an important manufacturing center of this country, I was also aware of the role and significance of the labor movement. From an early age, I was conscious of the link between the civil rights and the labor struggles.

I went to college just as the anti-war activity was peaking, and the struggle against the Vietnam War was at the center of a great movement. We questioned many aspects of the social and cultural fabric of society, but I always came back to the same point. The working people, in their great masses, must be at the center of any movement for change. Without the active involvement of the working class and broad masses of ordinary people, no real and lasting change can take place. Only this path will lead to a fairer and more just society. The labor movement provides this vehicle, because it is the self-conscious driver of the spontaneous aspirations of tens of millions of people.

This is the cause to which I have devoted my entire adult life. As an elected and an appointed leader of three separate unions over 35-plus years, I have done my best to advance the great cause of working people.

The document that follows is entitled "Blueprint for a New Western New York," and represents my values. I wrote it, but it is the product of three years of activity of the Western New York Area Labor Federation, AFL-CIO (WNYALF). It was adopted as a programmatic "working document" by our executive board in November of 2014. The concepts and theory outlined signify a synthesis of my hopes and a number of projects and policy initiatives of the years 2011-14.

While I am the author of this document, nothing at all could be put on paper and then used as a guide to our work without the active participation and sanction of the executive board and staff of the WNYALF, and as such, I simply wrote down what had been in operation for the period noted. The questions and positions taken may or may not be appropriate to other regions and areas of the state or country; actually, for the world. That is a question for others to consider. What it does signify is an attempt to answer certain vexing questions facing our labor movement.

There is no question that our economic, political, and social systems are in flux, and that real crises exist in all areas of life. The labor movement represents the best and most efficient form of organizational struggle of the working masses. This has been true for thousands of years. The division of society between rich and poor is the actual driving force behind most historical developments. In this country, the real struggle for the working masses has been to defend and extend economic and political rights. This holds true today, just as it has at other historical junctures. The struggle to end chattel slavery concluded in a bloody civil war, and continues today in the fight against racial discrimination, bigotry, and white supremacy. We are still fighting that battle. The fight for economic rights did not end with the industrial workers gaining union organization and the passage of the Wagner Act in the 1930s. We are still fighting it today; only, under changed and complicated circumstances. Other examples abound.

Today, our unions only make up about 11% of the total work-force, yet we actually have greater influence than those numbers indicate. The broad struggle for higher wages is an example of that influence. This issue is not just for those in unions; it extends way beyond to all those whose earnings have stagnated or been reduced during 35 years of trickle-down, "race to the bottom" economics. Organized labor must be champions of this fight; it is an imperative of the movement.

Further, our role does not stop with the question of wages, or wage disparity. The "Blueprint" is an attempt to analyze and lead a movement of ordinary people toward economic democracy. It is in the best traditions of the labor movement to do so.

Over my 35-plus years of activism in the labor movement, most recently as a Teamster leader and as the President of the Western New York Area Labor Federation, AFL-CIO, I have tried to provide a theoretical perspective. My interest in theoretical questions is not for academic purposes alone, although I suppose any time one delves into the realm of theory an academic angle goes with the territory. No, for me the real issue is not simply to understand the world, it is to change that same world. If this "Blueprint" helps in that pursuit, and provides for more and greater experimentation in pro-worker programs and policies, it will be for a very good cause indeed.

## Blueprint for a New Western New York.

The region is changing in dramatic ways. There is economic expansion, new industrial development, new occupations, expanded opportunity, and more wealth being created than at any time in over 40 years. This is not hyperbole. The population of Erie County and the City of Buffalo is actually increasing. There are thousands of people living in the extended downtown region, and unemployment is down while per capita income is showing signs of growth.

How is such a thing possible? After all, it was just six years ago that the economy went into a massive decline. The Great Recession, brought on by unprecedented and unwarranted speculation in the housing market, led to a crash, the likes of which the country had not seen since 1929. This region was hit hard, although not as hard as other parts of the country. Yet, here we are with real expansion, on a high-road basis. Seven years ago, forces that included various community groups and numerous unions defeated the Bass Pro project. It was replaced by the build-out of the inner harbor (including Harbor Place and other related projects), UB 2020 (University of Buffalo) and the medical school moving to the corridor, the expansion at Chevy Tonawanda, the expansion at Ford, the dramatic growth of the medical corridor, the industrial projects at the old Bethlehem Steel site, the SolarCity project, and many others. Further, the number of old buildings downtown being reused for housing and hotels is in the multiple dozens.

What confronts the labor movement and allied community-based organizations is, how can we participate in this growth without becoming "giddy with success", and without forgetting that our goals in this economy are not always necessarily in line with those of the business community? Clearly put, we have our own independent thinking and plan of action to ensure that this prosperity works for the broad masses of the laboring people.

### What We Believe
### 1. A Steadfast Defense of the Economic Rights of the Working People

The basis of unity and the core mission of our Labor Federation are standing as one against the shifting of the burden of the economic problems of society onto the backs of the working people. The issues of the stagnation of wages, worsening health and safety conditions, and healthcare and pension concerns are at the center of fighting for and maintaining a prosperous working class. We see the WNY Worker Center, a project of the Western New York Center for Occupational Health (WNYCOSH) as providing a crucial link to that part of the labor movement that is outside the formal structure of our affiliated unions. Further, we must aid those unions that are organizing new bargaining units in whatever manner is appropriate to those campaigns.

## 2. High-Road Economics

The WNYALF has consistently put forward a program geared to the development of high-road economics and good jobs. We support initiatives that are the opposite of the "race to the bottom" that has plagued this country for decades. We support jobs that pay a living wage, have benefits, seniority, and positive labor relations, whether they are union or not.

## 3. Subsidy Reform

Similarly, we are in favor of incentives that pursue high-road jobs, and have transparency and accountability. We are opposed to incentives that lead to a dead end, including most retail, doctors' and lawyers' offices, and any other schemes to put taxpayer dollars into the hands of developers, without real community improvements. The Coalition for Economic Justice has played a key role in this effort. For a decade, they have been fighting against the "race to the bottom" in economic development by demanding that government subsidies to business are accountable to real high-road economic growth.

## 4. Community Benefits

We want to make sure those communities, especially in the national minority neighborhoods, are not left out of this new economy. Community benefits must take into consideration people who have been consistently left out of positive economic growth.

We push for living wages, fair housing policies, and programs that address chronic and high levels of imprisonment. As part of this effort, we have worked to establish the Center for Occupational and Environmental Medicine (COEM), in collaboration with Erie County Medical Center (ECMC). COEM will serve the needs of the working population by providing needed services for those afflicted with debilitating diseases caused by pollution and other related industrial hazards. We look forward to continuing to work with the WNY Worker Center and the Coalition for Economic Justice to ensure that economic development works for the ordinary people. Further, we applaud and hope to strengthen ties with the VOICE-Buffalo organization, which has an active program aimed at keeping working- class youth out of prison.

### 5. Just Transitions

The reality of global warming is here. The polar ice caps are melting and the ocean levels are rising. Greenhouse gases have warmed up the planet, and the results are increasingly severe. This is a product of an economic crisis brought on by the interests of the oil and gas monopolies. It is a very serious threat to the health of the planet.

We are in favor of fighting this phenomenon without wiping out the jobs and livelihood of literally millions of workers. We are in favor of working with community groups to save jobs and make a transition to a non-fossil-based energy source, one that is paid for not by shifting the burden onto the workers and their communities but by a collaborative movement to find solutions. The opportunity for this work is ever-present, and with partners such as The Clean Air Coalition, we strive to form a bridge to the affected communities.

### 6. Progressive Political and Legislative Program

The forming of tactical alliances to achieve concrete legislative and political goals is an essential part of the economic and social concerns cited above. The alliance with political and governmental leaders as part of a united front to defend the working conditions and living standards of the great masses of the American people is not up for debate. The forces of the right wing of the Republican Party are on a path that could lead to an authoritarian political system, where the rights of the working people are trampled.

### 7. Social and Cultural Issues

A working-class culture cannot, almost by definition, be one dominated or heavily influenced by bigotry, racism, white supremacy, or any other forms of exploitation and oppression. Finding the means and methods to promote working-class solidarity with cultural and social programming is a valuable component of our movement. As part of this program, we will continue to promote positive, life-affirming values such as working-class solidarity, volunteerism, and service to the broad community.

Pursuing this program will contribute to the building of the new Buffalo in a way that will make us proud. We should redouble our efforts in this direction and put this region in the national spotlight.

My values became clear growing up; reading the biographies of leaders, observing Buffalo's troubles, and learning about the Civil Rights Movement, protesting the war in Vietnam, and identifying labor as the engine of progress, so I am grateful to have been able to contribute to economic and social justice through my professional life. I am especially proud to be working with the Western New York Area Labor Federation and our strategic partners to develop this Blueprint, to share it, and be using it to build a stronger community.

# WORKING STORIES

# LEADERSHIP NETWORKS

Melinda Mack

Many people say that leadership comes from somewhere outside. Some have argued that you have it innately, that you are hardwired, and fine-tune it with training. Leadership has to do with timing, a gut that has been informed by personal experiences, and having the right support network around you.

My own background shaped my leadership style: it is rooted in tenacity, deep empathy for those around me, and an unfettered curiosity. This has translated into an evolving set of skills that has helped me grow into the leader I am today. This also defines how I approach my work and my life.

I grew up just outside of Buffalo, born in the early '80s to parents who lived through the rise and decline of the "Queen City," the crown jewel of the state, second only to New York City. My Buffalo roots are deep, running through large middle-class ethnic families that value honest hard work and Sunday suppers. My passion for workforce development is rooted in my love of Buffalo. Long before politicians started to notice it, I had seen a beautiful, complicated city. This inspired insatiable curiosity that led me to take every single internship I could get; earn two graduate degrees, in Urban Planning and Public Administration; and travel to the far reaches of the world. This curiosity and need to create change led me to spend years learning and working to solve some of society's most complicated social issues. I deeply believe that most people in this world are good, useful, and underutilized. I feel a connection to the underdog nature of my hometown, and more importantly, the need to see the good in the city and its people.

I have also been shaped by my family's experiences. My mother's father was an entrepreneur, always scrabbling to keep afloat or to grow a range of enterprises. From men's clothing to light manufacturing, he strove to turn ideas into things, and then into profit. My grandfather on my dad's side was a "union man," an operating engineer, building some of the most recognizable structures across Western New York. In personality and presence, the two men could not have been more different—one in flashy suits, drinking Manhattans, and the other wearing work boots, with a Genesee Cream Ale in his hand. While they were remarkably different, the pride they took in their work, and their persistence, were common denominators.

However, as significant as my grandfathers' stories are to who I am, it is the stories of my grandmothers that have served as the basis for my inspiration. Both are smart, creative, and industrious, and raised five and seven kids, respectively, but it is not just their roles as mothers and grandmothers that define them. They've put themselves out on a limb, taken chances, and worked to defy the norms. They are compassionate, quick-witted, and organized, and have demonstrated immense empathy in some incredibly challenging circumstances. They are not only capable, but remarkable. I see many of their characteristics, most notably, empathy and openness to others, in myself and in my own parents.

Those who know me well can sense the undercurrent of urgency in all that I do. My mom was diagnosed with cancer for the first time when I was a teenager, and she was 39, just a few years older than I am now. Because of this, I grew up fast, and without the luxury of feeling invincible in my youth. As I watch my mom continue to fight, I know my time is limited. The result is that I struggle with complacency and feel a profound need to continuously march forward toward an ideal, even if I never get there. I am not easily fazed, and remain dedicated even when others start to falter. I don't see insurmountable challenges but, rather, the big, hairy stuff that builds our character and a puzzle that needs the right pieces or resources to be solved. I thrive in settings where I have huge, systemic issues to tackle—it just means more data, people, or puzzle pieces to fit together.

It wasn't until I began to work, and saw these big, hairy issues with my own two eyes, that I recalled a conversation I had at my grandmother's kitchen table. We'd been working on a middle-school project about careers, and I asked, "Granma, what did you want to be when you grew up?" She described her fascination with the women in the Air Force who helped build and test planes during World War II, and how she had dreamed of being one of those women. She spoke wistfully of traveling the world, being part of an effort that mattered, and doing something interesting. I was floored. I had only known my grandmother as a housewife. I asked why she hadn't pursued her dream, and questioned whether she should have tried harder. She tried to explain that it just wasn't in the cards for her. Even though she was a good student, she didn't graduate from high school; not because she didn't want to, but because her father didn't think it was something a woman needed to do, so she was pulled out just weeks before graduation. Hearing this, I remember feeling stunned. A combination of the creeping flush up my 12-year-old neck, and the apparently sudden hardness of the chair, made my skin tingle. I felt embarrassed, but I didn't know why. Was I embarrassed for her, or that I had even asked? How could a woman so smart, so charming, and with so much ambition be told that this was how things would be? How was her recent history so completely out of line with what I had been told my future would be?

I am part of the generation that immediately benefited from the women who demanded change. Those who came before me ensured that my grandmother's story wasn't the future for all young women in this country. This also means that I live in a kind of purgatory, as that generation which came immediately after the fight. For me, it meant that I had an unrealistic expectation that the world had changed and everyone was on board. I came of age after historic shifts like Title IX, the push for equal pay, the right to birth control, and the market demand for more college-educated women. In my youth, girls were told they could do anything. We could be astronauts and executives, or take on "non-traditional" jobs; as engineers, for example.

I also grew up in the era where *All in Family* and the *Mary Tyler Moore Show* were in syndication—both considered revolutionary at the time. One night, I watched the portrayal of a vibrant, single woman making her way and choosing career over a husband and family. Another night, it was Archie insulting Edith as a "dingbat," and America providing a pass to a "guy who was just afraid of change." Just think about the mixed messages; not just for young girls, but for everyone.

When I get to speak with the rare female executive who is nearing retirement, much of what we talk about are her experiences on the way to the top: the constant need to prove that one is an authentic leader, the need to be known as someone who can run with the "big dogs," make the tough decisions, and "hold one's own"—all without showing too much leg. These women dealt with constant sexism; so much so that it seemed like part of the job. They were called *shrews* and *bitches* when they were tough, and *girls* when they were emotional. They also talk about the sacrifices they have had to make when their careers had to be their priority, at the risk of losing it all. They talk about being out there on their own.

In the late 1990s, in some of my earliest work experiences, I was shocked at just how antagonistic the environment was toward women; even forward-thinking colleagues, including other women, just accepted it as the norm, or "part of the game." I can still vividly picture a colleague laughing at a horrific biased joke because she felt she had to. It took me a while to untangle the fact that this was not just an isolated "bad work environment." This kind of thing happens nearly everywhere, and to every woman, with varying degrees of intention. Now, in retrospect, with Archie Bunker and Mary Tyler Moore in our vast pop-culture archive, I should have anticipated the immensity of the challenge of unbraiding the current culture from the past.

In contrast to the women at the start of the women's movement, my generation grew up with moms who worked. Increasingly, they were college-educated, and in some cases, were women, like my mother, who had climbed the ladder in their careers. Now the rhetoric is about the new imbalance of highly educated women flooding the workplace, the power of the female consumer, the new definitions of traditional gender roles, and the work-life balance. However, despite all these gains, women are still at a loss. Women currently make up only 5.3 percent of the Fortune 1000 CEO positions, and the U.S. Congress is comprised of only 19 percent women representatives, even though more than 50 percent of the nation's population is female. I believe it comes down to a simple fact: women are still faced with, and then scrutinized for, making the decades-old choice. You can either sit at the head of the boardroom table or at the dinner table in the evening with your family. I don't want to have to make a choice like Mary Tyler Moore; I want to be a great mom and a great leader.

So, in addition to changing the outcomes for the underdogs of society, I also feel the need to live the change I want to see for women's equality, especially in the workplace. I feel as though I am constantly pushing the envelope to redefine norms, and it is exhausting. No longer should it be about the choices women make to "do it all" (and putting those choices on a stake in the courtyard for all to see), but about creating an adaptable work environment that increases productivity and allows for work-life balance. This means creating policies and practices that allow each employee to maximize their work and their life.

Because of who I am, and how my life and work experiences have shaped me, I refuse to keep quiet when I need to shout about things I care about, or to be defined by someone else or the world around me. Some have called this tenacity or youthful idealism; others call it stubbornness. For example, in eleventh grade, I shared that I didn't think my high school was adequately preparing me for college in a piece that ran in a local newspaper. I experienced a severe backlash from the teachers within the school, even though I was the president of my class and a good student. Over 10 years later, I worked on a Gates Foundation project specifically geared to increase the college readiness and success of high school students in New York City public schools. Even with the mounting pressure, I knew I was right; it just took me 10 years to prove it.

Looking around the field of workforce development from my perspective, I see another "Buffalo": a deeply important network of hardworking, underutilized gems that needs to reclaim its place in history. When I get up every morning, and think about what we do, I do not see us as a network of misfits or idealists. I see us as advocates; as the persistent drumbeat saying that we all matter, and that education and skills development are the great equalizers. There is a famous expression that says, "Luck is what happens when preparation meets opportunity." My organization ensures that New Yorkers have access to both preparation and opportunity.

The work our members do is hard, thankless, and often viewed as "tarnished" in some way. From the outside, some people don't view those we work with as good, useful, or underutilized. They see them as takers, slackers, and never good enough. They don't recognize that "those" people and local employers are part of their own community.

By now you know that this field is my life's work. This is not just a job for me; it is who I am and what I believe. I am engaged in complex, systematic change that makes my heart skip a beat. Many readers feel connected to this work the same way I do. You share my frustration with the pace at which the world is moving and the challenges we face. But our time is here. I need each of you to succeed. We need to translate the passion each of us has for helping people become great into propelling forward the change that will make our issues everyone's priority.

At the same time, let's balance our work lives with family and community. I am committed to my family, as they are to me. I have the incredible fortune of having amazing mentors and a supportive husband and family who will do whatever it takes to help me be successful. This means helping me find the elusive work-life balance. They step in and pick up the slack when my time or energy is waning, or reinforce what is going well inside and out of the office.

Without these supporters, I may not have had the stamina to keep it up my entire career. They remind me that doing meaningful work means working within boundaries to create change, but also taking risks to put what you believe on the line and push the goal posts back, even if it is excruciatingly slow. Most importantly, they remind me that anything worth changing can be changed, and I have to be that change—even if there is a backlash. When I think about how this translates into creating new norms, what I see is that new battle lines have to be drawn by my generation, especially as we try to coexist with the generations before us, and for those that follow.

# WORKING STORIES

# ON BECOMING A LEADER

Ed Murphy

*I would not be a Moses to lead you into the Promised
Land, because if I could lead you into it, someone else
could lead you out of it.*    —Eugene V. Debs

I am a reflective practitioner. I learn from reading, experience,
effort, success, and failure. Adaptation strengthens my capacity to
lead. Writing this essay is part of an external meditation.

I am a leader, focused on economic and social justice, ethics,
and organizational effectiveness. How do I know? Because I stepped
forward, articulated a vision, gathered support, listened, practiced,
studied, experimented, made mistakes, learned from them, found
coaches, applied for executive jobs, was hired, succeeded, and
gained confidence. One day, I knew I was in the guild.

Authentic leadership is not just a title. You earn it every day and
can lose the privilege. Someday my slot will be taken or handed over.
It may hurt, but I won't complain. I've had a good run. I hope these
reflections encourage younger labor leaders. That's one reason I'm
writing here. Another is to help me understand what I have done and
to focus on the next phase of my life.

I came to the New York State American Federation of Labor and
Congress of Industrial Organizations (NYS AFL-CIO) in 1999, with
diverse experiences and a reputation as an innovator and implement-

er. I was given opportunities, as well as financial and institutional support. A year later, I founded and became Executive Director of the Workforce Development Institute (WDI).

Leaders improvise. Sometimes they even make history. Gandhi did not have a blueprint. He titled his memoir *Gandhi, An Autobiography; The Story of My Experiments with Truth*. Life has no clear path. Leaders interpret trends, lean forward, point the way, seize the moment, take a risk, and encourage others to join them on a journey. There are no leaders without a constituency lending them authority. You have to respect those who invest, who give you power. Your role must be renewed, with humility, often at awkward moments. Think of a rubber band. You can only stretch a relationship so far. One end moves forward while the other holds you back. Push too far, too fast, and the band will break, and that is the end of your leadership. The best leaders stretch, introduce tension, educate, and inspire their constituency. Then the group follows and takes ownership of new ideas and relationships.

WDI was birthed by many, but my story is the one I know best. With a mixture of pride and humility, I share how I was prepared for my role. I ask you, the readers, to reflect on your own experiences and leadership; to accept credit for what each of you has contributed to your family, community, and country. I am proud of my leadership, and hope that you are of yours.

We built WDI with a clear focus: to serve working families and; to strengthen organized labor's voice and role in workforce, economic, and community development. I brought vision, skills, self-confidence, and faith that we would succeed. Others invested time, sweat equity, ideas, money, advocacy, and encouragement.

I wasn't born to lead. I am the baby of my family, number six. Even the cats and dogs didn't follow me. This may have been a stimulus to find some way to become visible. Ask any musician or athlete, and they will tell you that one has to find a niche, practice, seize the moment, practice, draw attention, practice, find models, show discipline, practice, learn from good coaches and find better ones who will push you beyond your limited dreams, adapt, practice, and develop a personal vision of victory. Success cannot be prescribed. We improvise, make our own luck, take advantage of trends, and exploit leadership vacuums.

I grew up Irish, with the clarity of the Roman Catholic Church and the confusion of my mother's death in 1952, before I was seven. My family was filled with grief. We focused on what was lost and how to survive. Pop took care of the basics. We kids became a team, with more autonomy than our peers. Our family offered love and support, and still does. This is one reason I have confidence, and value organization, teams, cooperation, and reliability. Religion gave me hope that someday I might see my mom again and that there is more to life than living. Public school gave me intellectual discipline.

I learned from three strong leaders. My father was the prime authority, provider, and unifying force. Our pastor, Father McCormick, ruled on Sundays and was an ever-present spiritual guide. Mrs. Cerreta, principal of Public School 11, was my secular authority. The family gave me a sense of organization and coherence. The church offered hope and inspiration. Grammar school trained my mind, demanded discipline, and provided skills. My leaders were confident and inspiring, fallible, and practical. I've met few better. Leadership is local and personal. One needs to understand and care about those who follow. As Che Guevara said, "The true revolutionary is guided by great feelings of love." There must be shared values and trust.

My yearning for, and focus on, transformative social change started when I was a wounded child. I wanted my life to be better. I found I wasn't the only one who needed help. Faith and education moved me beyond my family's impacted grief. Public school teachers showed me a world beyond religion. President Kennedy became my significant leader. I developed a relationship with him. He was Irish, Catholic, a Democrat, a war hero, and articulate. He challenged me: "Ask not what your country can do for you; ask what you can do for your country." The priesthood was my response. Paulist Father Kelly, another articulate and inspiring Irishman, spoke to my parish and pointed me toward his American religious community. In 1963, I left Staten Island for their seminary in Baltimore. I learned how to learn. My eyes and mind opened wider. Working among the inner-city poor showed me that many had it worse than I. We visited prisons. I walked along death row and through mental health wards. I spoke with drug addicts, and each night returned to a safe, white, quiet school; warm food and clean sheets; to priest-professors who committed their lives to service. We were privileged. I learned of worker-priests who shared the life of those they served. After three years, I realized that faith was a personal asset. My primary interest was in social and economic justice. I saw how religion could be a barrier. A comfortable clerical life protected me from having to take responsibility for my own survival. I remain grateful to the Paulist community for spiritual and academic education, training, support, and inspiration. In 1966, I decided it was time to move on and take responsibility for myself, to grow so I would be able to serve others. I had expanded my perspective. I trusted that God had work for me to do. But first I had to take off my training wheels.

Much happened in the following years that contributed to my understanding. Leaving the Paulists, I gave up my draft exemption. The military waited outside the novitiate. I engaged my fate, enlisted, became an intelligence agent, learned to speak Vietnamese, and went to war; a dramatic change.

I came home with a combat veteran's caste privilege. I was a Vietnam expert, and became an anti-war activist. I stood up for peace, organized with Vietnam Veterans Against the War (VVAW), and drew media attention. The press ordained me a leader. I accepted the role and title; helping other vets, talking to community groups, being on the radio and TV, getting my message out. Action was practical, comforting, and therapeutic.

I risked my life in Vietnam and survived; I have never taken that for granted. My new life began on May 9, 1969, when I came home from the war. I did not want anyone else to die. I risked my identity, security, and future when speaking out against the war, motivating some and antagonizing others. I got hate mail: "Your mother must be a Jew." Some said I was a traitor to my Irish race. "What did you expect?" my supportive father asked. He encouraged me to let this roll off my back. Instead, it showed me the connection between war, racism, poverty, and social and economic injustice. Many saw my standing up as an act of courage, yet it was more about integrity and responsibility.

I was a former combat intelligence agent, fluent in Vietnamese. I had frontline experience and solid information relevant to the public debate about our war. I didn't have a right to remain silent. Leadership requires personal integrity, vision, action, and humility. One needs to risk rejection and accept credit with humility. Vietnam drew me out. I had to either speak up, or be ashamed and live with my conscience. My expertise, caste privilege, and voice made me a leader. Standing up in my home community was a risk. I invited support and criticism from those who knew and loved me. I lost some friends and gained some more. A few family members were embarrassed. I sought help dealing with the emotional consequences of this. I came to understand how important it is for leaders to know themselves, to explore their personal feelings and motivations, and to respect the psychological dynamics inherent in conflict. Mental health is an asset, and asking for help is a start. I began to study all aspects of transformative social change. I sought further opportunities to serve, to learn, and to become more effective.

In 1970, I returned home to Staten Island. I'd been inspired by Gandhi, JFK, RFK, Dorothy Day, Martin Luther King, Jr., and Saul Alinsky, the great community organizer and author of *Rules for Radicals: A Pragmatic Primer for Realistic Radicals*. Alinsky spoke at a Paulist seminarians' conference, and encouraged young people to organize within their home communities, where we had shared history, experiences, and credibility.

When I left the army in Washington, D.C., I could have gone anywhere. I wanted to go home. I'd spent three years in seminary and three more in the military. Coming home from war, I was lost and needed to get grounded. I was angry and had a score to settle. Staten Island sent me to war. I'd enlisted and filled a draft slot in my community's quota. I wanted to have a community conversation about what that meant, and what I learned, reporting back to those I represented in Vietnam.

I also needed to complete my education. Most of my intelligence peers had undergraduate degrees; some, even law degrees. I had only two years of college and a weak academic record. I was hungry to learn, and wanted another chance. Richmond College (CUNY) gave this to me. I chose to live, study, and organize on Staten Island. I stood out, and was elected president of the student government. I helped focus the student body, and represented us to faculty, administrators, and our local community during turbulent times. I engaged in civil disobedience to protest the war. I was arrested at the White House with Linda Geary and other friends. Eighteen months later, Linda and I were married. Lin's feminism opened my eyes further: male leaders must listen to and respect women, disarm our sexist perspectives, learn from women, and advocate for their concerns as much as our own.

Two years later, I defeated our congressman to become a delegate to the 1972 Democratic Convention. In that process, I tested myself against a neighbor, a distinguished West Point graduate, Korean War hero, and experienced elected leader. I learned two important lessons. Every leader is vulnerable, and a well-organized insurgent with a good cause and field operation can win against traditional complacent leaders who behave as if elected office is their right.

At the Miami convention, I had a rude awakening with the media. My prior experiences with journalists had been positive. Reporters asked good questions, took notes, and fairly represented what I said. I was an interesting interviewee: a former combat intelligence agent who spoke Vietnamese, who had served in an infantry division, and who had exposed the CIA's Phoenix Program as a reckless assassination initiative. At the Miami convention, it was different. The national media had already framed their story: another Chicago. They had less interest in who I was and what I knew. CBS national correspondent John Hart saw me as another anti-war veteran inside the convention, while a contingent from VVAW demonstrated outside. He asked about my commitment to George McGovern and what we would do if the Democrats didn't nominate him. I didn't plan on losing that fight, so I did not give an answer. He pushed, and I said, "We will do what we have to if we face that situation." Hart became intense, and asked, "Are you threatening violence?" His story was about crazy Vietnam veterans rather than me, a combat veteran who rejected violence and was working inside the system to make change. I looked at him like he was crazy, but he was serious. My values were clear, but they conflicted with his storyline.

The day Bobby Kennedy was killed, I was at war, and had shared my perspective in a letter to my brother: "Vietnam is one of our mistakes.... In our country there are many ways to make ourselves heard. I hope the legitimate means afforded us through the democratic process will be used. If the swifter and more dramatic means of violence are used, then history will have that much more reason to condemn us."

If Hart had been interested, I would have explained that I had committed myself to nonviolent direct action. I was insulted by his assumption that veterans were dangerous. He taught me to be careful with my answers; to understand who I was talking to, and to be clear about my messages and what reporters wanted out of each conversation. Hart had his story and he just needed a comment from me to justify his assumptions. He had seen the 1968 Chicago convention, expected a replay, and was ready for a scoop. I learned again that if I wanted to communicate messages, I needed to be clear, concise, and prepared for smart, stupid, and insulting questions. I also had to get better at presenting my perspective.

At home, my interests expanded. Freedom for Northern Ireland, environmental advocacy, and interracial justice became concerns. I made connections between an immoral, wasteful war and the destruction of the environment; between a foreign policy that supported dictators in Vietnam, Chile and British colonialism; between racism at home and abroad and our preference for killing instead of providing jobs and healthcare.

In 1973, I ran as the progressive candidate for Borough President of Staten Island in a Democratic primary. I advocated for veterans, peace, healthcare, the environment, civil rights, fair housing, and to close Willowbrook State School, but I did not understand public finance. Had I won, I would have faced New York City's fiscal crisis and yielded to more conservative technocrats to make the trains run on time.

I chose to develop executive skills, and did my apprenticeship in San Diego. Lin was accepted to graduate school in Psychology, so we moved west. I became director of an agency serving the poor and the homeless. Our staff was made up of young counterculture activists. Six weeks after I was hired, 129 businesses petitioned to have the agency defunded. They saw us as a magnet for the homeless, and objected to our clients walking their streets, sleeping on the beaches, and disrupting the tourist trade. My mission impossible was to reorganize the agency, rebuild community support, and convince county government to continue funding us. I used skills I didn't know I had and found an organizational mentor. Anne Dosher taught organizational development at Lin's graduate school, and was a neighbor and founder of my agency. She said, "It's a good thing that you are sane and not looking to make a career out of this job."Anne saw that I was an East Coast guy, and believed I would return east after Lin graduated. She explained that an organization reflects the psychological profile of its leader. Previous directors had wanted to run a club: to be friends with their staff and clients rather than lead an effective organization that helps people. I prioritized services, success, and survival of the agency. I was willing to direct, compromise, and develop partnerships with the business community, rather than lead a cultural conflict. We all won. And Anne was right. Lin graduated and we moved to Saratoga Springs, New York.

Richard Nelson Bolle's *What Color is Your Parachute* helped me prioritize where and how I wanted to live as much as it helped me with finding work. Lin and I had grown up on Staten Island. I'd left for seminary before the bridge to Brooklyn brought urban life and "paved paradise and put up a parking lot." I liked being near the City but separate too. We chose to live in Upstate New York so I could work in state government. We arrived without jobs. My first one there was in a state park inside Saratoga Springs, a small city north of Albany, with an easy commute to the state capital. In 1976, having found work, I started graduate school in Public Administration. I studied government while practicing it.

My career path has been varied and full. I've learned from all I've done. Every four years, more or less, my jobs changed. By 1981, I had a Master's degree and a new baby, and had lost my job, so Lin and I founded Pathfinders Institute, a non-profit. We led initiatives related to PTSD: veterans, rape crisis, and domestic violence. We built an agency from scratch.

In 1983, I went back into government, joining Governor Mario M. Cuomo's administration to develop programs for Vietnam veterans, while Lin ran Pathfinders. I learned to integrate policy, programs, budgets, and personnel. In 1987, I moved from the Division of Veterans Affairs to the Civil Service Department, and was invited to lead development of the state's first workforce plan. In 1991, I returned to Vietnam for a United Nations Industrial Development Organization (UNIDO) investors' forum to explore economic development opportunities. I had hurt Vietnam; I wanted to help heal her and rebuild America's relationship with her. This was deeply personal, and an opportunity for me to use my intelligence and language, my political and organizational skills. It was a unique and time-limited opportunity, so I returned home and got myself out of government. Lin supported my decision.

I left steady State employment to start another business, Murphy Associates, a small consulting group. With a mortgage and two children, we took another risk, not wanting to miss the historic opportunity to work on reconciliation between America and Vietnam. I did business consulting, environmental, and humanitarian work. I wrote about Vietnam, spoke at colleges, produced three photography exhibits, and produced a book with our daughter, Zoeann: *Vietnam: Our Father Daughter Journey*.

These experiences prepared me for a 1999 invitation I received from our friend Denis Hughes when he was elected President of the NYS AFL-CIO. Denis invited me to become part of his team. I stood at a crossroads. Lin and I had considered moving to Vietnam, where I would have more opportunities as a business consultant. We decided it was not in the best interests of the family, especially for our children. Vietnam had been isolated by an embargo for decades after our war, and their schools were not very good. Four years earlier, I had run for mayor of Saratoga Springs, and almost won. I was planning a second campaign. I was confident I could win, but victory came with a $14,000-a-year salary. Denis's offer was not fully defined, but there were many pluses: working for a man I respected, staying in our community, our children attending good schools, an opportunity to serve working families, strengthening organized labor, a real salary and benefits. I had organized veterans, developed services, and contributed toward reconciliation with Vietnam. I'd done my share and needed economic stability. I chose organized labor. A colleague ran for mayor in my place and he won. We both won.

Authentic leadership emerges from personal experience. It balances personal and constituency needs, and engages in a dynamic relationship with those we lead and learn from. I did not emerge through traditional union ranks, so I had to earn my right to lead. I listened, learning what was important to union members and labor leaders, and I found a niche. WDI became where I could add value. Denis hired me to participate in his renewal of organized labor. I partnered with his secretary-treasurer, Paul Cole; legislative director, Ed Donnelly; and Joe McDermott, the director of the Consortium for Worker Education (CWE).

Together we incubated WDI as a vehicle to assist the statewide labor movement. I am a non-profit entrepreneur. We recruited a strong board of directors and founded WDI, and I became its director. My first priority was to listen and learn. I visited regional labor leaders and heard their priorities. We decided to expand the mission: to serve working families; provide incumbent worker education and training services; and strengthen relationships with businesses, minorities, women, immigrants, and community groups.

Through graduate education in public administration, work inside government, and running non-profits and a small consulting group, I learned the New York State procurement process. My first accomplishment at WDI was to show how New York State Education Department funding for union training could be realigned to give organized labor more influence over state training resources. Unions were approaching schools with a tin cup, begging for funds for training. I designed an initiative that enabled statewide education funds to be contracted through CWE to WDI and distributed to unions. This let local unions design their own courses and gave WDI operating resources. I demonstrated my value and earned the confidence of labor leaders. The legislature increased our funding, and we grew beyond union training to provide child care, business and economic development, and cultural and community services. We strengthened our regional operations. Local advocates communicated their satisfaction to legislators. They saw how effective we were and they renewed and enlarged our appropriations. We built strategic partnerships with organized labor, legislators, the business community, educators, and community organizations.

Self-responsibility and credibility are twin aspects of good leadership. Fiscal impropriety breaks faith and trumps the best intentions. I see myself and WDI as trustees of public funds. We built WDI with strong and transparent fiscal controls. In the murky and practical world of government, our reputation for fiscal integrity became an asset. Denis brought me into organized labor. My behavior had to reflect his ethics and good judgment. I needed to not shame him. Many more have since invested in my leadership, provided financing and organizational support, and accepted my guidance.

I must be proactive, responsive, and fiscally responsible in order to remain credible. WDI documents programs and processes, requires double signatures on all checks, has annual external audits, and promotes transparency. I managed inside government, ran non-profits and a small business. I'd put my family's security on the line. I understand cash-flow management and how vulnerable a labor group could be to allegations of fiscal impropriety. As Anne Dosher pointed out to me, an agency reflects the personality and integrity of its leader.

So, what now? I believe in succession planning. I am getting older. Someone needs to take my job, and I am not qualified to decide who that will be. Like most leaders, my perspective is constrained by my own experience. My goal is to help the next generation of leaders, not choose one. There are no blueprints—only examples, hope, principles, and experiments. I am a reflective practitioner, so I recommend that emerging leaders step forward and start with an environmental scan: study yourself, your organization, your society, and then design your own strategy. I was born in 1945 and defined a leader in 1970. I grew up during the Cold War, studied in a seminary, became an intelligence agent, went to war, and came home on a mission to build a nonviolent, peaceful, and just society. My generation's social environment included an economic resurgence, war, racism, sexism, homophobia, a concentration camp for the "mentally retarded" (Willowbrook), activists, inspiring leaders, and what President Eisenhower called the military-industrial complex, which partnered with Congress and universities.

We have made progress: ended the Vietnam War, built an environmental movement, and improved the lives and rights of women and gays. We closed Willowbrook and integrated developmentally disabled citizens into society. We finally have national healthcare. We still have war, racism, and the military-industrial-congressional complex. Workers, unions, and immigrants are under siege.

The next generation of leaders has plenty to do. They will push their own priorities, using newer and more appropriate technologies. I did not grow up with computers, cell phones, the Internet, Facebook, or even seat belts. Younger leaders have intuitive knowledge I am missing. But I am a futurist and an optimist. I have great confidence in the next generation, and write, offering to help. I share the path I took as a contribution, a reference, but not a map. I believe the most important skill an emerging leader needs is an internal guidance system, a combination of values and ethics, and a personal GPS and gyroscope.

In 2014, I signed a five-year non-renewable contract with WDI. My primary purpose is to lead the agency and strengthen its capacity to operate without me. There is a body of literature about what happens to an organization when the founder leaves. The best founders prepare their organization, surrender willingly, encourage change, and don't try to manage from the grave. We each have our role and our personhood. It is best to understand the distinction. I am no longer building an organization. We won. I am writing more and mentoring. The best thing I have done for WDI lately is to hire strong leaders, capable of managing independently. I don't agree with all of their decisions, but they can't lead if they only obey. I won't let go in years to come if I don't practice now. I am also engaging my board more in wide-ranging discussions related to mission, services, and direction. Boards get comfortable with, and support, a strong and skilled executive. I need to continually examine that balance and partnership. We have an informed and strong board, skilled leadership, and regional and administrative teams. We have built a leader-full organization. My role is to clearly state a vision, encourage everyone's strengths, guide the agency, and develop younger leaders who will refocus WDI to address emerging trends.

I feel responsibility to the field of leadership. I invite comments and discussion. I write because I must—in order to stay clear and discuss what I believe. I respond to those who ask questions, listen, challenge, corroborate, and help me learn.

Thanks for listening. Please share your perspective with me at emurphy@wdiny.org.

# WORKING STORIES

# MEANINGFUL WORK

## Lin Murphy

*Behind the sometimes seemingly random or even
chaotic succession of events in our lives as well as in
the world lies concealed the unfolding of a higher order
and purpose.*

> —Eckhart Tolle, *A New Earth: Awakening to
> Your Life's Purpose*

Sometimes we learn what is meaningful to us by finding out
what isn't.

Finding our place in the world of work is not a straight line. It's a
winding road, with peaks and valleys; with yield, stop, and go signs.
It changes, depending on where you go and the people you meet
along the way.

Most of us start thinking about careers toward the end of high
school. In my case, I was thinking about being a gym teacher. Gym
was my favorite class. I was happiest when I could jump around and
move my body. I was the captain of the cheerleaders, and I loved to
dance, surf, ski, play tennis, and do anything else that let me expend
an overabundance of teenage energy.

After researching programs in Physical Education, I found out
from my parents that there was no money for college. That summer, my dreams were dashed, but I didn't give up on finding a way
to get educated and finding a career that I enjoyed. That setback

gave me time to question becoming a gym teacher. My own gym teacher blew a whistle and gave directions, but did not participate in the activities themselves.

I had a boyfriend at the time who was bound for medical school, so I started thinking about doing something in the medical field. I found a program in medical technology at the local community college.

I spent two years studying organic chemistry, math, and biology, and learning how to run medical tests, which involved a lot of mathematical calculation.

While doing an internship in a hospital, I learned that there were two things I did not enjoy and did not want to be doing for work: math and sitting at a lab table all day long. I gave up medical technology, and also the boyfriend.

Neither was right for me. The boyfriend was always criticizing me and wanting to shape me into someone I wasn't and am not, and I was attempting to please him. This is a recipe for misery. Still, breaking up is never easy, and I felt lost. After spending a summer in San Diego, California, attempting to find myself, I enrolled in Richmond College, the City University of New York—a working-class college. The majority of the students were enrolled in practical business and engineering programs. At the same time, college campuses across the country were on fire with political activism.

I spent much of my time at the Staten Island Peace Coalition, organizing to end the war in Vietnam. I learned a lot about politics and community organizing.

In the '60s, everything was up for grabs. New programs, such as Women's Studies and Integrated Studies, were being introduced. There were breakthroughs in science and quantum physics. We were young, the music was amazing, and we believed we could change the world. I had an adviser who believed in, and encouraged, me.

This freedom of thought was new to me, coming out as I was from a conservative working-class family. My parents lived through the Depression. What was important to them was having enough work to provide food, clothing, and shelter; certainly not lofty ideals, like meaning, purpose, and creating social change.

During my college years, I met dedicated, spirited, and courageous people. We were passionate. Our large-scale opposition to the war in Vietnam helped to end it. We were engaged in a massive shift in consciousness across every field and institution, and it was thrilling to be a part of it.

I met Ed Murphy at Richmond College during training in nonviolence and civil disobedience. We were preparing for a protest in Washington, D.C., against the Vietnam War. Ed had returned from military service in Vietnam and came to Richmond College to earn a degree. He was the president of the student body, and an outspoken critic of the war. Ed and I became life partners. We shared values and we had fun together. We were both rebels, and enjoyed skipping class to go for a ride on the Staten Island Ferry.

During this tumultuous time as a student, I found that I enjoyed studying human behavior. I took courses in psychology and pathology, as well as leadership development and organizational change.

I graduated with a Bachelor's degree in Psychology and went on to California for a Master's degree in Community Psychology. Ed and I founded a non-profit organization called Pathfinders Institute. We wanted to continue to work on projects related to peace and non-violence, and to help people find their path to peace. We developed one of the first programs to treat Post-Traumatic Stress Disorder (PTSD) before it was even recognized by the medical community.

After a long career as director of Pathfinders Institute, counseling Vietnam veterans with PTSD, and other victims of trauma, I transitioned into the new field of Transformational Life Coaching.

Coaching uses the analogy of a sports coach, but applied to the game of life. The purpose is to help people reach their full potential and overcome beliefs and actions that sabotage their desires, plans, and dreams. I trained with the world-class Coaches Training Institute. I use a co-active model, which means that the process is a dialogue about what works, and how to have effective relationships. I don't tell people what they should do with their lives. I ask powerful questions to help people discern what's meaningful to them.

The focus of my coaching is wellness and balancing work and life.

I had a long-term dream to start a holistic health center with like-minded colleagues, so I helped found One Roof Holistic Health Center in Saratoga Springs, New York. The town is famous for its "Health, History, Horses." There is a famous racetrack, but also mineral springs and a spa, where people come from all over the world to drink and soak in the natural spring waters.

My office is in a beautiful old Victorian house, furnished with antiques and beautiful Turkish rugs. The colors are soft and soothing, and people comment that they feel better just walking in the door. They come to heal trauma, manage stress, and find more meaning and balance.

As I age, I'm now fascinated with this new leg of the journey. I want to learn about it, while I experience new challenges and spiritual opportunities. How do we age with grace? I facilitate a program in "Conscious Aging," where a group of elders can explore and write about issues of aging and death.

As a psychotherapist, life coach, and change agent, here are some things I've learned about meaning in work: What makes work meaningful is different for each of us; there is no one definition; our purpose is constantly evolving as we try things out, meet people, learn new things, and travel to new places.

Any job can be meaningful. The question is, "What makes you come alive?"

Here is what some of my clients say about what makes them excited about their work:

"I get to share my inherent gifts and talents—I am creative and naturally good at music and art. I need to create to thrive."

"I'm able to make a positive impact on the lives of others; I volunteer for an organization that is helping one village in Kenya to build a school. It gives me satisfaction to know I'm making a difference in the lives of the neediest kids on our planet."

"I'm a stay-at-home mom for now, and I wouldn't have it any

other way."

"I work hard and am rewarded well. I'm able to provide for my family. That makes me feel good."

''When I am fully engaged and am acknowledged for my work by my employer."

We have a purpose when we say *yes* to what is ours to do and *no* to what is not ours to do. Many feel stuck in a job that they hate and are only doing it for the paycheck or benefits. This is true of many state workers, where the institution stifles creativity and initiative, and they feel buried in rules, regulations, and paperwork.

In my generation, we were encouraged to be practical and to choose work based on its ability to provide security and financial stability only, rather than seeing it as an opportunity for alignment with our passions and dreams. We did away with arranged marriages, and should have a new vision for our livelihood.

One visionary, Matthew Fox, author of *The Reinvention of Work*, refers to "The Great Work" of the universe. We are all part of one unifying spirit that moves through us for the good of all. When we are aligned with this force, we are doing what we love and serving the whole.

We are not just cogs in a machine, meant to push paper and produce things that we don't need, or that do damage to ourselves and our environment.

Rosabeth Moss Kanter, a professor at Harvard Business School, said in a recent Harvard Business Review:

"Great companies identify something larger than transactions for business portfolios to provide purpose and meaning. Meaning-making is a central function of leaders, and purpose gives coherence to the organization.

Meaning-making is understanding what makes employees tick and creating environments where people can make a brilliant difference."

If you're doing something consistent with who you are and your values, then you're on track. If you're not, you can change.

A client of mine named Bill came in with the following story:

"My father was a lawyer and he wanted me to be a lawyer and eventually take over his firm, so I did.

I feel like I'm in the wrong field and never stopped to think what it was that I wanted. I can't change now... I have student loans and a mortgage, and I'm stuck."

I reminded Bill that it is important to remember that you are never trapped in a job or a career, despite how it seems. Once he believed this, we worked to find options.

He continued part-time with his law practice while he pursued his passion for fitness and wellness. He is now a personal trainer, and is enjoying his new career. Bill was able to make a transition into another career where he felt more aligned with what he did 40 hours a week.

When discussing meaningful work, we have to talk about values.

Getting clear on your values and then exploring how you are or are not honoring them is a pathway to success. For example, most women value relationships highly, in and out of work. I enjoy networking, having conversations with clients about their hopes and fears, and talking about possibilities. It comes naturally.

Being clear about your values, and then expressing them through your work and relationships, creates fulfillment. But finding work that matters isn't always easy. Sometimes, a job is just a job. We work to earn money to pay our bills.

A single mom with no skills may work one or more minimum-wage jobs to feed her kids. This is necessary and honorable.

Fulfillment can come from doing what you love in other areas of life. Life is not all about work, after all.

For example, I often hear, "I want to be a writer," and everyone I know wants to write a book. The standard joke is "keep your day job".

When I ask, "Are you writing?" and I hear, "Yes, I write every chance I get, because I must," then I encourage this person to explore the possibilities of earning a living from her writing. Otherwise, I tell her to write for pleasure.

Meaning and happiness do not come from making money alone.

There are billionaires who are not happy.

Every human being has value, regardless of the size of their paycheck or their job. People find meaning in all sorts of places other than work: in their families and relationships, playing sports, working for political candidates to help get them elected, church, book clubs, travel, or volunteering, to name just a few.

Here are a few questions to consider:
- What is it that I most deeply desire to experience in life?
- What is it that I most deeply desire to express in life?
- What is it that I most deeply desire to create in life?
- What is it that I most deeply desire to contribute to life?

Meaningful work is subjective. It is different for every one of us.

I have discussed some commonalities in this essay. We are able to use our innate gifts and develop the skills we need along the way. Meaningful work is bigger than the way we make our living. Meaning comes not only from our jobs but from other parts of our life, such as our health, relationships, environment, and spiritual and personal growth.

We find meaning when our work is bigger than ourselves and we feel connected to a larger cause, when what we do is aligned with our values and unique purpose, and when we are making a contribution that benefits others.

# WORKING STORIES

# CONSIDER PUBLIC SERVICE

## Paul D. Shatsoff

With government under seemingly constant fire from so many quarters, it is a wonder that anyone with a choice would opt for a public-sector career. However, in spite of the scandals, administrative failures, and inefficiencies, I believe government tends to work pretty well, thanks to the millions of women and men who choose it for a career. As of 2012, there are 22 million public employees in the United States; 16 million of whom work in education.

For more than three decades, I devoted my work-life to public service. There was no single event that led me to a public-sector career, but a combination of experiences and the desire to make a difference in the lives of other people. The saying that a public servant "works for the people" sometimes gets lost in the day-to-day shuffle of paperwork and deliberations that are part of any government. Though I chose public service for the meaning and difference it could make, most of the positions I held were administrative or executive, but I looked for opportunities to add more meaning to my job.

The most enjoyable and rewarding period of my career was when I was on the adjunct faculty for a graduate program in public administration. I would open the first class of each semester with a question: "Why did you choose to pursue a public service career?" The answers from year to year had little variation. The most common answers were, "I want to make a difference in people's lives" and "I want to get meaning out of my work."

There were a number of other answers too, such as, "I couldn't get into the MBA program," or "I didn't know what else to do." Or, "I thought it would give me steady employment and good benefits." Not surprisingly, no one said they did it to get rich.

Public servants do their jobs every day, mostly without any special recognition. They work so that people can have better lives, can live in a safe environment, can get help in times of need, and more. Though elected officials are in the public-policy spotlight, government couldn't do its job without the unelected professionals who have chosen public service. Public-policy implementation would not happen. It is important to highlight the value and meaning of public service, so that it becomes a career choice for many of our best and brightest young people.

Everyone who enters government service has their own reason and story. For some, it's just a job. For others, it's a life mission. A close friend of mine who grew up in Massachusetts told me that he was influenced by the Kennedys, most of whom chose some form of public service. President John Kennedy's inaugural quote, "Ask not what your country can do for you; ask what you can do for your country," was especially influential to many young people during the 1960s, and continues to inspire in the 21st century.

My earliest interest in government is traceable to a radio program. Growing up in the blue-collar city of Bridgeport, Connecticut, I was interested in politics from the time I was 11 years old. I used to fall asleep at night with a transistor radio under my pillow, listening to a political talk show on NBC broadcast from New York City. My family never traveled far, except the 60 miles from Bridgeport to the Bronx, where the rest of our family lived. The radio, for me, was the gateway to places I never went or people I never would be likely to meet. I didn't feel deprived. I just thought that's how life was. I was lucky to have this small radio and a supply of batteries to power it.

In high school, I became involved in political campaigns as a volunteer; most notably, the campaigns of Connecticut Senator Abraham Ribicoff and, in college, the presidential campaign of

George McGovern. My real fascination was with foreign policy, and in college, that's pretty much what I studied, except for the required number of electives. In the turbulent 1960s and early 1970s, I began to study the origins of the Vietnam War, by looking into the history and politics of the region. This led to my participation in anti-war protests on campus. I was hardly what could be categorized as a "radical," but history and policy analysis told me that the U.S. and its allies had reneged on a promise that was made to Vietnam to support nationhood after World War II if the Vietnamese helped fight the Japanese. The Vietnamese held up their end of the bargain, but the U.S. and its allies did not, and chose to restore the French to rule their former colony. This decision was shaped, in large part, by the post-war distrust of Russia and its allies, and a fear that communism would spread to all of Asia and beyond. Cold War politics prevailed over Vietnamese statehood.

I became discouraged with the anti-war movement on campus as it fragmented and gave way to more radical groups that I did not agree with, whose agenda extended beyond ending the war. One day, I participated in the takeover of a building on campus where some students were trying to attend class. We used to take over buildings as a sign of protest. Some of the takeovers were more symbolic than others. This was the case with of the Reserve Officers' Training School (ROTC) building, which was occupied by student protesters and painted inside with larger-than-life cartoon characters, intended to create an image that countered the building's purpose as a training facility for the military that was conducting the war.

One day, I marched into the School of Engineering building with a group of protesters. The students in the engineering program were science-and-math-oriented, and generally not thought by us to be interested in politics. These were the students who wore small leather pouches that housed their slide rules (precursors to scientific calculators and personal computers). They thought that going to class was more important than ending the war, so we set out to disrupt their learning, and change their minds.

As we stood in the back of the room, shouting to interrupt the class, it struck me that, as much as I had a right to protest outside of the building, the students who wanted to go to class had that right as well. This, coupled with the radical fringe that began to take over the student movement on our campus, led me to leave the anti-war demonstration. I lowered my protest sign, turned around and exited the classroom, and then the building. Back in my dorm room with a six-pack of beer, I drank until I fell asleep. I remember removing an anti-war banner painted in red on a white sheet that I had hung outside of my dormitory window. It read, "Shatz Says End the War Now!" I was depressed.

The way that the war was handled made me more interested in becoming involved in government. Maybe in some small way, I could be an influence for better, more informed, decisions. I now realize there is a certain naïveté in this thinking, because government policy is often heavily influenced by politics, at the expense of pragmatic, rational assessments. This should be understood as a fact of life in a government-service career, not a deterrent for pursuing it.

In the aftermath of Vietnam, and knowing that the war could have been avoided, I began to think about a career in the Foreign Service. Though my interest in government began while listening to a radio talk show, I never seriously considered running for political office. In politics, you are always asking people for something (usually money), and I was never good at that. As a volunteer during one campaign, I was asked to be part of a phone bank to solicit donations. I pleaded with the campaign organizers to assign me to any other task. They obliged my request.

My desire to enter the Foreign Service changed during my senior year. A visiting professor, on leave from the Central Intelligence Agency, taught my American foreign-policy class and took an interest in me.

One day, the professor/CIA analyst asked me whether I had ever considered a career in public administration. I had to admit to him that I didn't know exactly what that was, since I had been so focused on foreign policy for over three years. Having gotten to know me a little bit over the course of the semester, he thought public administration might be a good fit, where I could act out some of my desires to make government serve people better. He sent me to see a professor of Public Administration at the university, and we had a long talk. Though I had been thinking about public service as a career for a long time, I never thought of this service as being in the domestic United States. So this was all new to me.

Sometimes where you end up is more accidental than deliberate. I completed graduate school with a Master's in Public Administration, intent on working for a town or city government somewhere in New England. This level of government was closest to the people, and appealed to me. One of my professors encouraged our class to apply for one of two public administration internships in the country; the first was in Phoenix, Arizona, which had an excellent reputation for training its public administrators, and the other was the State of New York's Public Management Internship (PMI) Program. For a kid who grew up traveling no farther than from Bridgeport, Connecticut, to the Bronx and back, I decided that Phoenix might put my family (and me) into shock and despair. I applied to the State of New York program and, in March, I was called in for an interview at the World Trade Center in New York City. It was a strange format, because there were two of us in the room who were being interviewed simultaneously. We were both asked the same questions by a small panel of interviewers. My counterpart had several years of relevant work experience, and I had none. His answers were very direct and very New York-specific. Mine were a little more theoretical and somewhat general. I left discouraged, but since I wanted to work for local government anyway, I told myself it really didn't matter. Plus, I'd gotten to go to New York City and see the World Trade Center, which was a big deal for me.

A few weeks later, I got the call saying that I had been selected. It was a career path to a professional position within New York State government in Albany. I remember asking the person who called if they knew they were talking to Shatsoff, and not Shapiro, who was the other person being interviewed with me. The voice on the phone said it was Shatsoff they were looking for. I was in disbelief. I would have hired Shapiro.

My plan was to complete the two-year internship and then return to New England to pursue a career in local government. And where, exactly, was Albany anyway? I thought it must be someplace north of the Bronx.

People decide to work in government for their own reasons. You would not want government programs administered by people who chose their profession as a career of last resort. It is important to send a message that government service is worthwhile and can provide meaning that is not easy to find elsewhere.

I worked with people who made a difference every day. The governor may issue an executive order, but someone else implements its provisions. Regulatory commissions make determinations, but it is left up to career public servants to implement and monitor them. The courts set parameters or issue consent decrees that government programs must operate by. It takes competent civil servants to implement the courts' wishes. The same is true with programs established by legislatures.

When I was teaching graduate school, I began the first class with a conversation about examples of government intervening to make our lives safer and better. I pointed out that the paint on the walls was non-toxic because some government program determined that there must be standards for paint. The wiring for the lighting and electrical outlets was safe because of a government regulation. The food from the vending machines that the students ate during breaks had to meet the Department of Agriculture's standards. Cars, buses, trains, and planes all have to meet safety requirements that are prescribed by government, and its employees are responsible for bringing order to society in many ways. Some of this is mundane, but important nevertheless.

I like the example given in James Carville's book We're Right, They're Wrong. He describes his first encounter with a government employee, and writes: ''The first person ever to slap me on the ass was a federal employee. He was the army doctor at Fort Benning, Georgia, who brought me into this world." Government employees make a difference in the lives of all Americans, in a time of dire need and mostly out of the spotlight.

Carville expresses his opinion that those who are most critical of government often turn to it when they are in trouble. Think of automobile companies that lobby against higher mileage standards or against cleaner emissions and other forms of government regulation. These companies turned to government for help when their businesses were threatened with bankruptcy.

When the Affordable Care Act (ACA) was being debated, there were daily demonstrations outside the Capitol in Washington, D.C. I witnessed people carrying signs that said "We don't want socialism." Members of the same group also had signs that said, "Don't touch my Medicare," which is a form of socialized health-care coverage. My guess is that there was someone in that crowd who had a family member who was at some point denied health insurance because of a pre-existing condition, but they failed to connect their experience with what the ACA was proposing to do.

Sometimes when you work in government, you have to work hard to remain engaged. For example, as a budget examiner, early in my career, I volunteered to participate in a field study of methadone maintenance clinics in the New York City area. This had nothing to do with my actual duties, but it broadened my view of how government programs can help people in need.

In 1975, we were gearing up for the Bicentennial celebration of the United States. I had only been in state government for a year. During that time, New York State and New York City faced one of the worst fiscal crises ever. A bond default was looming. The City threatened to drag the State down the fiscal sinkhole. A front-page headline in the *New York Daily News*, referring to a speech by President Ford in which he denied Federal assistance to the City, read, "Ford to City: Drop Dead." (The president never used those actual words, but they captured the essence of his policy toward New York.) Working for the New York State Division of the Budget, my colleagues and I were tasked with cutting unnecessary expenditures from the state budget. I decided to look for some low-hanging budget fruit.

In preparation for the nation's Bicentennial, the State was funding a barge, which was widely supported by various patriotic groups. The cost of operating the barge and outfitting it with memorabilia of the Revolutionary War was over $1 million, which, in 1975, were big bucks. The barge would sail around the state on rivers and canals, and once the celebrations were over, it would be dismantled. In my view (a rather naïve one, I was to learn), I thought this would be a logical budget cut, and recommended just that.

My recommendation made it to the Budget Front Office. Word got out to the public that the barge might be cut. Remember my earlier point about politics versus rational policy assessment? Interest groups, like the Daughters of the American Revolution, mobilized. During a meeting of high-level budget supervisors which was attended by Governor Hugh Carey, the governor entered the room and opened the meeting by thanking everyone for their suggested cuts, but conveyed that he didn't want to hear any more about eliminating the Bicentennial barge. I was crushed. How could this be? Politics often trumps bureaucratic logic. A footnote to the story: after the Bicentennial celebration ended, the barge was dismantled and sold for a pittance to a salvage company.

During the millennium change, many computer programs that state operations depended on were so old that, when these programs were written, the date field only went as high as 1999. When the year 2000 arrived, what would happen to national defense systems? There were unfounded rumors that, in the federal government, which faced a similar problem with its computer systems, nuclear missiles would self-launch. What about the banking system or the checks that people depended on to pay their bills and buy their food? Would these systems crash at the stroke of midnight in the year 2000? Would air traffic control systems work? Would some terror group take advantage of the disarray to cause more chaos? Many of the programmers who were the authors of computer codes that contained date instructions were either retired or dead. Government agencies tried to track them down. Documentation had been misplaced or not prepared in the first place, so fixes would be very difficult, if not impossible. There was a real sense of fear inside and outside of government. I recall being in a meeting with state agency commissioners who were introduced to the millennial date issue for the first time. A shock and awe-type speech was given to them, because the year 2000 was a deadline that could not be altered. They needed to address this right away. At the time, it seemed very scary.

In New York State, a government task force was assembled to prepare for the possible consequences of the millennial date change. I was part of that task force. We went through a number of simulated catastrophes that might occur. The task force would meet regularly in a bunker deep below the ground. The bunker was originally built during the Cold War and had a massive steel door that could effectively seal it from an atomic blast. The door, I was told, hadn't been tested in decades, but there was something frightening about its appearance and original purpose.

A number of state agency representatives worked extremely hard to prevent computer meltdowns as the year 2000 approached. I was witness to government at its best, even if the worst fears of computer meltdowns came true. As the date change got closer, these people worked round-the-clock to modify existing systems or write entirely new codes.

The night of the date change, while most New Yorkers were celebrating New Year's Eve, a few hundred public employees were in the bunker and at other locations in New York State, just in case. There were no major consequences. The morning of January 1, 2000, brought a sense of relief in the bunker.

During the terrorist attacks on the World Trade Center in 2001, the world was able to witness public employees in action during and after the attacks, some of whom lost their lives. I witnessed an act that was not generally visible in the aftermath of the attacks. Because the explosions were so horrific, the remains of many who died were never identified, including a member of my own family. For weeks after the incident, the survivors of those public employees who had died waited for survivor benefits to be paid. However, because in many cases there was no evidence of death, no death certificate could be issued. Without a death certificate, survivor benefits could not be paid. A person with whom I worked took it upon himself to bring this to its logical conclusion through tireless negotiations with state agencies, such as the Health Department and the State Comptroller's Office. The death certificates were issued and the benefits paid.

Every day, public employees are called on to prevent and deal with disasters in order to protect and serve the public. Much of this service is routine, but it gets done, and the public is well-served.

I am Chair of the New York State Academy for Public Administration. Four years ago, we decided to begin a Public Service Excellence Award Program. These awards illustrate, educate, and inspire people who wonder whether public service, as a career choice, can be meaningful.

A State Department of Environmental Conservation engineer, with 38 years of public service, oversees flood-control projects in the Southern Tier, and played a key role in saving lives and property during and after the major flooding caused by Tropical Storm Lee. This employee is responsible for over 30 flood-control projects, consisting of 52 miles of waterways, 17.5 miles of levees, three miles of floodwall, 179 gates, and a large dam. His work was described as extraordinary, and despite record flooding during Tropical Storm Lee, there was no loss of life in his sector. He also volunteered and assisted several communities on Long Island after Hurricane Sandy. His floodplain management experience was invaluable.

On March 12, 2014, there was a huge gas explosion in East Harlem that destroyed two large apartment buildings. Eight lives were lost and several people were injured. There was also damage to several other buildings because of the explosion. One of the first responders was an investigative team from the New York State Department of Public Service who had to work among the rubble and in very confined spaces to determine the cause of the explosion. The employees maintained their composure when faced with the tragedy they found. Over many weeks, this investigative team worked long hours at the site; 14- and 16-hour days, and many without overtime pay. Others postponed planned vacations. The teamwork and excellence they displayed during this ordeal is a noteworthy example of public service.

Healthcare is one of the most costly expenses of state and local governments in New York. A county attorney decided to take initiative and use his expertise to make changes in a small county's prescription drug program, which resulted in $11 million in annual savings while simultaneously improving the program. His ingenuity was a win-win for the employees of the county and the taxpayers, and he did it on his own initiative.

Also at the county level, a career public servant was given an award for his leadership in spearheading a waste-to-energy project at a sewage treatment plant, which saved the ratepayers nearly $500,000 annually in energy costs by converting sewage sludge to energy. The project also involved reclamation of wastewater in the sewer district to be used as cooling water for the treatment plant. This saves the county seven million gallons of fresh water each year.

From human services, from child-abuse hotlines to senior services, from disaster relief to collecting taxes, from inspecting roads and bridges to finding cures for our worst diseases, public service offers countless opportunities for meaningful work that can make a difference. It's not always easy, but the intrinsic rewards can be great.

It will take a new generation of quality leaders and program managers at every level of government to solve the known and as-yet-unknown challenges of this state and country. As public administrators, the challenge is to find ways to tell the stories of what government employees accomplish day-to-day. Their work touches all of our lives in many ways, though we rarely realize it or think about it. The message that a career in government is a desirable, worthwhile, and honorable choice needs to resonate early on with students in our schools. Public service needs the best talent that this country has to offer.

# WORKING STORIES

# ACQUIRING YOUR VOICE

## Bob Trouskie

This essay examines how I acquired my voice; one meant to promote social, legislative, and practical changes in the effort to assist working families. Mostly, this essay is a self-reflective account of my life, with emphasis placed on my family upbringing, working career, educational background, mentorship, age, and experience, as well as other pertinent activities that helped me develop the voice I now have to promote change.

Ten years ago, I was counting the days to retirement at General Motors. If I had been asked then to write a description of the ideal job for the next phase of my career, it wouldn't have been better than my current position at the Workforce Development Institute (WDI). So how did I get here? At 60 years old, recognizing that I'm nearing the end of my working career, I now have the credibility, experience, and appropriate platforms to use my voice. When reading my story, I want you, the reader, to ask yourself: How did you get there? What life and career events shaped your belief systems and enabled you to acquire your voice to promote social change?

### Family Upbringing

I was brought up in a middle-class family that placed a very high emphasis on working hard and never missing a day of work. At a recent family function, my 73-year-old brother mentioned that he hadn't taken a sick day in 52 years with the same company. I don't remember my mother or father ever taking a day off because of illness. If you had a job, you had an obligation to go to work, regardless of how you felt. My parents didn't have a lot of extra money, and from an early age I was always encouraged to make my own. I had lawn and snow-shoveling customers at age 12; I had a morning paper route from ages 12 to 18; I worked multiple afternoon and weekend jobs during my high school years. "Anything to make a buck" was the phrase my family used when describing me. Those jobs developed the work ethic I maintain today. Yet they also limited my participation in school activities, including sports, clubs, and other things that make for a full and well-rounded educational experience. Even though I attended a private Catholic high school that emphasized attending college after graduation, I was one of a small handful who decided to immediately start a career. That decision was okay with my family, as they placed little value on attending college. I'm the only member of my family who ended up attending, and graduating from, college, albeit as an adult student. My wife's family, on the other hand, placed a high value on attending college. My wife and four of her five siblings attended, and graduated with professional degrees.

## Working Career

I started working at a stone quarry immediately after graduating high school. Over my seven years there, I was promoted a number of times to better-paying positions and given additional responsibilities. I received those promotions solely through my hard work and commitment to the company. I started to realize that the credibility I had as a worker also brought with it more opportunity to give my opinion about operations. I found I had a meaningful voice that most people listened to.

In one case, though, it took the intervention of a third party to have my voice heard. It was 1973, and the recently formed OSHA was going to inspect the quarry for the first time. I drove a quarry truck at the time. These trucks were huge and hauled rocks and boulders from one section of the quarry to a primary crusher that ground up the rocks into smaller sizes. On a typical day, 40 trips were made to the crusher, each with 35 tons of rock in the bed of the truck, down a very steep road inside the quarry. Since starting to drive the truck the year prior, I had told the company mechanics that the brakes would not stop me when going down the hill fully loaded. They dismissed my concern by saying that when they drove years ago, their trucks didn't stop either, and that I should feel lucky, because those trucks didn't even have doors or workable heaters. The OSHA inspector chose to ride with me, and the first time down the hill, he asked me to stop the truck. I tried, and it wouldn't stop; it didn't even slow down much. He asked me to try pulling up the emergency brake, which I did, and the truck kept going. After I dumped that load of stone in the crusher, the inspector asked me to get out of the truck. He asked me what I would have done if a pickup truck or car had been stopped in front of me on the hill. I replied that I would probably have driven over it. He then called the garage; a mechanic came down and drove the truck up the hill. That afternoon, I was allowed to drive the truck again. The brakes worked. In fact, they worked every day after as well. To this day, I don't believe there was any malicious intent on the part of the mechanics having me and others drive trucks with faulty brakes; rather, it was just the way it had always been. What I learned was that having one's voice heard sometimes needs the assistance of a third party who either has more credibility; or in this case, sanctioning authority.

After leaving the stone quarry, I took a job at General Motors, where I started working on the assembly line. I quickly discovered that seniority was a key element to a worker's advancement, GM being a union shop, in contrast to the non-union stone quarry. That never swayed my work ethic and commitment. I was there every day, giving my 100%, regardless of the job. My hard work was recognized by the union leadership, who asked me to run for union office after being there only a few years. I never aspired to be a union representative; in fact, my family all worked non-union jobs, and the few times that unions were brought up around the dinner table, the discussion was usually negative; addressing a strike or how much union workers got paid. I accepted the new role totally unaware of what I was getting myself into. I felt awkward at first wearing a union-representative shirt, but it soon became apparent that the shirt gave me the responsibility of not only expressing my own voice, but also expressing the voice of the union leadership, as well as the voices of the members whom I now represented. The shirt was but a symbol, however; my credibility as an effective voice had to be earned from others, including union leadership, members, and management, through hard work, integrity, fairness, visibility, and genuine interest in and concern for others' issues. I'm proud that I never lost any of my five elections.

One phrase I never wanted to hear from any of the members I represented was "the only time I seem to see you is during election time." The reason I never heard that term is because I made it a daily practice to see and interact with all of the 250 members I represented. By doing so, I demonstrated that 1cared about their issues and concerns. The daily interaction also enabled me to be a more effective voice, and to better represent their concerns. It was challenging, seeing everyone daily, but one of the fruits of that labor was an unblemished election record.

Other union roles I eventually had gave me the opportunity to challenge myself to grow as a person, become a leader, and, ultimately, acquire a respected voice with the entire union membership and leadership, as well as the company leadership. Those roles also gave me the opportunity to work with community and educational groups outside the plant to develop programs to assist the membership. It was slightly uncomfortable at first meeting with community and educational leaders, but I discovered they were interested in what I had to say. I possessed something they did not have: the practical experience and knowledge of the workforce. My voice became a critical ingredient in the development of numerous programs that were eventually offered to our workers. Two of those programs were the Paid Educational Leave (PEL), where union members attended college full-time, and the Technical Educational Preparation (TEP), where members attended college-prep classes 40 hours a week in order to acquire the skills needed to enter the PEL program the following semester. Both programs were designed so that members could focus on their education, while simultaneously receiving 100% of company pay and benefits. The design and implementation of both programs involved countless meetings with secondary education and college administrators who were very accustomed to operating programs in prescribed manners, such as semester start and end dates, the amount of credits needed to be classified as a full-time student, and the amount of hours their teachers could work. Each item was an issue, but not one was insurmountable. Through dialogue and compromise, the needs of the school and union-member student were both taken into account and the programs were created.

The development of both programs enabled me to establish relationships with educational providers and community leaders that I still have today. Many of those long standing relationships are still very important to have with activities I'm currently engaged with as the Director of Field Services for the Workforce Development Institute. Two other by-products came from the development and implementation of those programs. First, it gave me the incentive to pursue my own college education through night school. Second, it enabled me to positively change people's lives.

### Educational Background

Never ashamed for not choosing to attend college upon completion of high school, I did gradually find that the lack of a college degree limited my career options. Laid off from GM for just over a year in the early 1980s, it was almost impossible to find another quality job, solely based on being a hard worker, with only a high school diploma. When I was recalled to GM based on my seniority, I immediately worked as much overtime as possible to save up for the next time I'd be laid off. I felt like a gerbil in a spinning wheel; preparing for the inevitable, but not really changing my situation. The opportunity to develop the college and pre-college programs for the union members altered my focus to include my own education as a means to eventually break the cycle of either being laid off or working 12 hours a day, 7 days a week.

Using the night-school approach and starting with one course a semester, I eventually increased my workload, taking two and sometimes three courses per semester. I knew it would be a long road, but I enjoyed the learning, the challenge, and having something in common with the other union members who were taking college classes in programs I oversaw. Another by-product of being in night school for 14 years was the genuine support and encouragement from the same college staff, educational providers, and community leaders I had been working with to design programs or meeting with during other community boards or functions. At every meeting or event, at least one person would ask how school was going, and offer their encouragement that I continue and finish. Those words of encouragement helped keep my morale high and my desire to succeed intact.

My ultimate educational goal was to earn an MBA. To follow that path, I received an AS in Business Administration, and was deciding what two courses to take to finish up my BS degree in Business, Management, and Economics. One of the final courses I decided to take was in Adult Education. That course, coupled with my interaction with adult learners, totally changed my direction. Instead of attaining a business degree, I focused on eventually attaining my MS in Adult Education. I found that this was an area I was truly passionate about, and it also provided me with a number of future opportunities to exercise a strong and knowledgeable voice to assist others.

## Changing People's Lives

Acquiring a credible voice puts one in a situation to assist others make positive changes to their lives. I really cannot imagine anything more rewarding and humbling than being part of improving another's situation. Through my working career, two instances stand out: one was unexpected and instantaneous, while the other happened over a period of time.

The first occurred with a union member whom I represented for years. He was around my age; a very vocal, boisterous, and intimidating guy. Always in and out of trouble at the workplace. I had many occasions of representing him during disciplinary procedures. As the college PEL and pre-college TEP educational programs were recruiting students, I encouraged him a few times to give one of them a try. His response was always the same: "What do I need college for; I have a job?" After the third or fourth time I discussed the program with him, he finally confided that he was scared that he didn't have the ability to go to school and be successful. With my encouragement, he decided to give it a try, and enrolled. About a year later, he and his son were participating in the same adult/junior bowling league as my son and me. He came over and said he wanted to introduce me to his parents, who were watching us bowl. "Mom and Dad, I'd like to introduce you to the guy who changed my life." That introduction happened almost 30 years ago. I can still remember the tone of his voice, the grateful look on his parents' faces, and the humbling feelings I experienced. My knees actually buckled slightly. That introduction truly reinforced the fact that I could make a difference.

The second situation happened as a result of a program I was asked to develop and teach immediately after retiring from General Motors. The Director of Adult Education for the Rochester City School District had heard I was going to be retiring and invited me to lunch. He asked if I would be interested in developing and teaching a training program to city residents, predominately single mothers who were receiving various social benefits. The focus of the program was to give them the skills and behaviors to get and maintain a job. I accepted the job and developed the three-week behavioral training program. I discovered on the first day of the program that I had never worked with students whose economic situation was totally different than mine. A way to illustrate that contrast: If my car breaks down, I'd either get it fixed or buy another car. My students, on the other hand, didn't have cars, and if they lost their bus passes, their lives were put into a tailspin. During my 18 months teaching that program, dozens of students would come into my classroom with huge smiles to report they had found a job. They were genuinely thankful for the instruction I had delivered and support I'd given. Those groups of ladies worked the hardest to succeed, and of all the groups I'd worked with, they were the most grateful for my assistance. Those students gave me an awareness of the problems faced by those who lack basic resources and, in many instances, a sustainable support system. On a personal note, that opportunity helped me become a stronger voice and advocate for individuals in different socioeconomic situations.

## Mentors

I think we've all had people in our lives whom we've considered mentors. It could be a father, working with his child in the workshop; a mother, teaching her child how to cook; or a neighbor, teaching a child how to play baseball. During my working career, I knew many individuals whom I considered mentors. None of them ever overtly took me under their wing; rather, they conducted themselves in a certain fashion that I learned from and wanted to emulate.

The first was the president of the Local union (UAW) I worked for at General Motors. He used to say it only took two things to be an effective leader: "Surround yourself with good and talented people; then utilize them." He was never one to solely accept the accolades and praises of a successful contract, program, or event; he always acknowledged the hard work of those who were behind the scenes, putting things together and making them work. He saw something in me early on and gave me the opportunity to become involved, grow, and acquire a voice representing the interests of the membership. When he was eventually promoted to the international union, his leadership philosophy was followed by his successor.

The second of the people I consider mentors was a gentleman who worked for the New York State Education Department. He is probably the smartest and most confident person I have ever worked with. He had the ability to pull together various pieces, align them, and, ultimately, structure a workable program. It seemed that, regardless of how nebulous his ideas seemed at first, he had the ability to bring those ideas to fruition. He taught me how to take complex issues and boil them down into workable solutions. He always took the time to explain to me the flexibility and nuances needed to have multiple agencies buy in and work together.

In addition, he introduced me to many of the people and agencies that I still work with. His job duties of representing a large geographical region were very similar to those of WDl regional directors. In fact, the current job description of a WDI regional director can be traced back to him. When I started with the WDI, the vision of having a statewide presence was in its infancy. The original model of brick and mortar training centers was morphing into something new. The previous relationship I had with him gave me the confidence to offer a new model to WDI leadership. That model was accepted, and different regional director duties and expectations were implemented.

## Age and Experience

While this may not be a requirement in every situation, I believe that age and experience were two building blocks that assisted me in acquiring my voice. Age has brought with it countless relationships made over the years. In many cases, those relationships assisted in forming alliances and coalitions that produced a powerful collective voice. My experience adds to my credibility. When meeting with a company, I mention the fact that I worked in a factory for 30 years. When meeting with a union, I mention that I was a union representative for 28 years. When meeting with a political leader, I mention that I was chairperson of a political action committee. By mentioning selected segments of my background, I can quickly establish that I have practical knowledge of the topic being discussed. Usually, conversations about mutual acquaintances or experiences follow. These, as well as describing my background, help me establish credibility, mutual understanding, and, hopefully, a rapport. Once established, it is much easier to have my voice heard and my ideas seriously considered.

I have found that my voice has been taken more seriously later in my career. I believe my age and past experiences, along with the confidence of having practical knowledge of the subject being discussed, helps me establish credibility. Without credibility, one's voice is viewed as mere noise in the background, and not taken seriously. In order to enact change, one's voice needs to be taken seriously and respected.

## Conclusion

Acquiring one's voice may occur through a set of circumstances, through a natural progression of one's life, or through a focused, systematic, laid-out plan. I would suggest that it occurs through a combination of these. With my own story, would I have accepted running for union office to become a third-party voice if the OSHA inspector had not decided to drive with me that day in the stone quarry? Would I have the same work ethic if I had been born into a different family? Would my career have progressed without watching and emulating people I viewed as mentors? Would I appreciate and value my education as much if I had attended college immediately after high school? Would I have continued 14 long years of college night school without the support and encouragement of my wife and others? Would I be as able to promote social and economic justice for others without the 18 months I spent teaching single mothers? Would I have accepted a job offer to work for the WDI if I didn't have my collection of life experiences? Some outcomes were planned. Some outcomes were happenstance. Collectively, all are factors in making me who I am today.

As I mentioned in the beginning, this essay has been a mostly self-reflective account of my working career. It is an exercise that I had never thought of doing. It has helped reinforce who I am, what I believe, and the difference I have made. It has also given me focus and the confidence to continue making a difference. Self-reflection is not an activity most of us take the time to engage in; we focus on today, tomorrow, and the future. I suggest that everybody take the time to look back at their careers and examine the events and situations that created the opportunities they found to use their voice. Having the credibility, experience, and platform to use your voice is the culmination of many factors in your career. It is something that should be appreciated and celebrated. Regardless of how finding your voice was achieved, you ultimately decide if and how it will be used. Having that voice is only the first part; you must also be willing to use it.

# SEEKING ALBANY JUSTICE

Richard Winsten

I write this essay as a lobbyist. I write about a legislative campaign to help New York pension funds to recover asset value losses
suffered due to financial fraud. The campaign fell far short of its
goals but did achieve at least one success, in the form of a compromise. I explain why. I also describe the legislative process that takes
a lobbyist through the highs of winning incremental victories and
knowing that the legislation's merits are right. I also describe ultimately losing and compromising more often than winning, which is
a regularly felt low for anyone who truly believes in what he or she
is advocating. It is important to examine failures in lobby campaigns as well as successes so that I can better benefit my present
and future clients.

My job is to represent clients and advocate on their behalf, not
mine. Ironically, in order to write here about these clients' views,
I must interject my own opinions, emotions, disappointments, and
hopes—the very things that I must avoid in my work on a day-to-
day basis.

Since finishing law school in 1978, my career has involved lobbying Albany, mainly on behalf of private and public sector unions,
as well as not-for-profits that support the work of these unions. I have
been fortunate to make a career of advocating on behalf of working
people. Their concerns are also my personal concerns. I have been
able to make a living and advocate for those whose voices often go

unheard, such as domestic and farm workers.

I found organized labor by chance. I had a vague sense that unions might be advocating for things I believed in. I interned at the State Assembly during the summer of 1976 and met the newly hired political director for the American Federation of State, County and Municipal Employees (AFSCME) at District Council 37. He was a political scientist who was looking for a law student to help him interpret the legal jargon in legislation. He hired me part-time in 1977, the year in which public employee unions won an agency shop law in Albany which provided that non-union members had to pay a fee in lieu of dues to their union because the union had the duty to bargain on behalf of non-members as well as members.

Some unions rewarded their lobbyists with the extra union income from agency fees with better cars and living conditions in Albany. My boss asked to hire me as legislative counsel. I was hired, and worked full-time for DC 37 until 1984, when I became the legislative and research director for the New York State American Federation of Labor and Congress of Industrial Organizations (AFL-CIO), which represents both the private and public sectors. I held that position up until 1987, when I founded the now quarter-century-old lobbying practice at my current law firm, Meyer, Suozzi, English, & Klein.

Key to my longevity in this lobbying career has been my ability to build credibility and trust with policy makers and with the groups for which I work. A lobbyist can play fast and loose with the truth and may be successful in doing so, but only on a one-off basis. To build a long career, a lobbyist needs to build trust and a good reputation. I always maintained the longer view; I have wanted to be known as a lobbyist who brings facts, honesty, and political sensitivity to my work with policymakers and longtime loyal clients. I have also tried to be very practical about what types of victories are feasible within a given timetable, since Albany mostly engages in incremental, rather than sweeping, change.

Nonetheless, the occasional opportunity comes when I can bring an issue to my client's attention that could be a "home run."

The Martin Act was one such. The trust and reputation I had built with unions in New York State allowed me to present the issue and to engage unions in support of a campaign to enact legislation. My urgings probably would have fallen on deaf ears on this legally complicated issue but for my good reputation and the battle scars I had already received working three decades for incremental change to benefit working New Yorkers. It is one thing to advocate for half a million or a million dollars for a program to benefit workers, and quite another to advocate for billions in restitution to the pension funds that hold the deferred wages of thousands of workers. Unions were supportive. They saw that this was a practical campaign with a defined legislative goal that could produce massive restitution to their pension funds. If successful, the work of the legislation could lead to the rare Albany "home run" for the advocates.

What follows is one lobbyist's view—that is to say, it is not a comprehensive review of the legal, policy, and political impact of the 2007-09 financial crisis on New York's public pension funds.

I was privileged to be able to play a role in this campaign directly, as a lobbyist for two public employee unions: Local 237 of the Teamsters and Local 1180 of the Communications Workers of America. These unions supported my analysis of the pension issue and my proposed solutions. This is different than the way most lobbyists get an assignment from their client and then go to work on the client's predetermined solution. In the course of building a coalition in support of legislation, I worked closely with many other public and private sector unions in New York State whose members were defrauded, and who had to pay the price for it in reduced pension benefits, as well as at the collective bargaining table. I received invaluable help, advice, and support from the New York State AFL-CIO and representatives of affiliate members who shared my view that there might be a chance to achieve restitution to pension funds for losses due to the fraud that caused, and permeated, the 2008 financial crisis.

I don't name names to blame. The importance of this article lies in its view of governmental and financial institutions, not of individuals who act in good faith to represent these institutions. However, there were two fundamental views of the behavior of the financial services industry: First, that blame can be fixed and compensation sought; and second, that the world of finance is too big to fail (TBTF) and too complicated to blame. If there was a near repeat of the Great Depression, it was because "shit happens," leaving unacknowledged the American consumers who lost $11 trillion in the value of their savings and homes because of Wall Street fraud.

I describe a lobbying effort to amend the New York State Securities Consumer Protection Law, called the Martin Act, in order to overcome legal obstacles to New York's public and private sector pension funds and receive civil monetary compensation for the asset value losses attributable to fraud that permeated the behavior of major financial institutions. The Martin Act was enacted in 1921 as a deterrent against securities fraud. It allows New York's attorney general to pursue criminal or civil charges against companies. But the law does not require the government to show proof that the defendant intended to defraud anyone, or that fraud actually took place. So the State has a lower bar to bring cases.

Attorneys general can use the law to seek an enormous amount of information from businesses based in New York, and they can also disclose an unusually large amount of information about their investigations.

Even without the proposed changes to the Martin Act, New York's attorneys general, Andrew Cuomo and Eric Schneiderman have utilized the Martin Act to address this fraud, particularly with respect to mortgage-backed securities that might have been held by pension funds. For example, Attorney General Cuomo issued Martin Act subpoenas to Bear Stearns, Deutsche Bank, Morgan Stanley, Lehman, and Merrill Lynch. Attorney General Schneiderman launched an investigation into bundled mortgages by Bank of America Corp., Goldman Sachs Group Inc., and Morgan Stanley.

This article points to work that remains to be done—putting the same power and resources to work at compensating New York pension funds, particularly the public funds.

The consequences to these pension funds and their members

were direct and immediate. In 2012, public employee pension bene-fits were cut for those newly hired. Public employers have suffered geometric increases in their pension contribution rates. Private sector union pension funds lost asset value, and the unions and employ-ers had to deal with the consequences in collective bargaining. The amounts lost are staggering: a hundred billion for New York's public pension funds alone between 2007 and 2009. Because the losses were so large, and because the consequences were so immediate, this was a high-stakes campaign.

I usually have very limited time to get my argument and task across to lawmakers and staff. I have to compress complex and technical material into sound bites. Of course, when the material is public pensions and securities law, the compression required is no mean feat: "The misdeeds of too-big-to-fail banks caused massive asset value losses to the New York public pension funds from 07-09. Efforts to recover these losses under federal securities laws are thwarted by the almost insurmountable legal barriers to recovery. New York's Martin Act would allow recovery under a more reason-able and New York court-approved standard. The only entity that can bring a Martin Act suit is the New York State Attorney General. The New York State Attorney General has done great work in recovering for injured homeowners but *de minimis* for New York public pension funds. This bill will encourage efforts on behalf of New York public pension funds to win restitution for the massive asset value loss."

The financial crisis has lain low both the national and New York economies. The crisis and its aftermath have had many complex moving parts and causes. However, the bottom line is simple, like the Star Wars struggle between Good and Evil.

In 2007, securities fraud and greed brought the Second Great Depression to New York, just as they did the first Great Depression in the 1930s. Banks used our pension funds to gamble in a legalized casino for speculators and they lost big, bringing down the whole economy. They were aided and abetted by securities credit-rating agencies that rated worthless junk as Triple A investments.

Bernie Madoff became a household name associated with financial crime. But his crimes paled in dollar value and harm committed by the Too Big to Fail (TBTF) banks. We all know how the economy has suffered: double-digit unemployment, the near collapse of the auto industry, and foreclosures.

In the second great bank Depression, two major investment banks self-destructed. Worse, it led to the $13 trillion bailout of the financial industry, while leaving the same old banking and invest-ment structures intact. Even the former Federal Reserve Bank Chair-man, Alan Greenspan, has admitted that a substantial cause of the financial crisis was "just plain fraud."

Trade unions' ability to achieve wage increases, health benefits, and retirement security depends heavily on the state of the economy and the investment performance of employers and employee pension funds. The fraud committed by TBTF banks that began in 2006, and which threw the economy into a tailspin from which it has not yet recovered, has made it harder for the unions and employers to meet the needs of middle-class workers.

The public employee unions and their employers are not to blame—those who defrauded our pension funds are to blame. To date, government treasuries and mortgage consumers have benefited by $37 billion in settlements, while New York pension funds have not recovered anything resembling the scope of their asset value losses.

The fraudsters should be made to repay the pension funds from their bonuses and stock dividends. The stolen money has not evapo-rated; it is there in Wall Street pockets to be reclaimed. All the TBTF banks have enormous litigation reserves that have been used to com-pensate nearly all injured parties except the New York public pension funds. The securities industry has reported record profits, and is once again distributing large bonuses. Just for those who work in New York City, bonuses at Wall Street securities firms in 2009 were $20.3 billion, up 17 percent from the year before, while New York public pension funds lost over $100 billion in asset value from 2006-2009, and about $300 million of that loss was just from AIG, Citigroup, and Bank of America stock. A report by City Comptroller William Thompson on behalf of the five New York City public funds pointed out that, from 2001-2010, City pension contributions rose from $1.2 billion to $7.7 billion. Further, the report concluded that 48 percent of the increase in City contributions was due to poor investment performance, particularly the 2007-09 meltdown.

I was privileged to work on a legislative solution to benefit public and initially private pension funds in New York State. Two unions in particular (Local 237 of the Teamsters and Communications Workers Local 1180) supported me and gave me standing as a lobbyist to advocate on their behalf. Initially, I worked on legislation to make it possible to sue, under the Martin Act, large institutional investors, public or private.

The Brodsky (A.8646)/Schneiderman (S.5768) bill was introduced in Albany in 2009. The Assembly sponsor was Richard Brodsky of Westchester, a veteran lawyer and legislator, and Chair of the Assembly Codes Committee. The Senate sponsor was then-State Senator, now-Attorney General, Eric Schneiderman. Both were members of a Democratic majority in their respective Houses and the governor was David Paterson, also a Democrat. Since the New York State Legislature is majority-party controlled, since the Democrats had that control, and since our sponsors were senior Democrats, the bill had a strong foundation. Despite committed and technically savvy sponsors, widespread support from public and private sector labor, the bill failed. Incidentally, a similar bill had passed the Assembly 148-0 in 2007. Its Senate counterpart was sponsored by Republican State Senator Thomas Libous of Binghamton and was reported from the Senate Committee on Corporations and Public Authorities, but did not get a Senate floor vote, and died on the Senate-floor calendar.

This legislation is necessary simply because the federal securities laws and the New York State Martin Act do not provide justice for our pension funds. The federal securities laws that used to provide that justice were enacted after the first Great Depression. In the 1980s and '90s, politicians gutted these laws at the request of the TBTF banks. This is not to suggest that nothing has been accomplished by the New York State Common Retirement Fund under the federal securities laws. The Fund did recover $624 million in a settlement with Countrywide Financial, later absorbed by Bank of America. This shows how egregious the Countrywide behavior was.

The negative attitude of Governor Paterson was captured in an article about his speech at the Museum of American Finance at 48 Wall Street: "The health of our financial sector directly affects the economic security of people in all corners of New York State." In 2007, Wall Street finances provided 22 percent of the revenues in New York; more than one out of every five dollars in wages comes from Wall Street. Wall Street capital allows for what is on Main Street—small businesses creating jobs. Paterson said Americans are understandably angry at Wall Street, but there needs to be "an understanding that Wall Street is the engine of New York's economy." He noted that other states have stood behind their iconic industries—the grape growers for California, the car makers in Michigan—and said New York should do the same. Paterson said, "You don't hear anybody in Maryland complaining about crab cakes. If you say anything about corn in Iowa, they'll run you out of town. If you say anything about oil in Texas, they'll string you up on the nearest tree. We need to stand behind our engine of economy in New York, and that engine is Wall Street."

Clearly, the bill faced strong headwinds from the governor, the head of the Democratic Party and usually a big influence on Democrats in the Legislature. The bill was also strongly opposed by the American Tort Reform Association and the Securities Industry and Financial Markets Association.

"Extending the Martin Act as proposed would make New York a magnet for class-action lawsuits against the companies that are the engine of our state economy," Kathryn Wylde, president and chief executive officer of the Partnership for New York City, a network of business leaders concerned with economic development, said in a statement, "This bill would drive away current and future corporate operations and could cause the loss of thousands of jobs and millions of dollars in tax revenues. There is little the state could do that would have such a negative impact on New York's ability to attract and retain business."

The Securities Industry and Financial Markets Association lobbying group said in 2008 that the "proposed legislation is unnecessary, duplicative, anti-competitive and harmful to both our national securities law policy and the stability of our markets and financial institutions."

So why did the effort take a step back from Assembly passage in 2007 to no passage in 2009? My view is that the intensity of the campaign waged by the opponents overwhelmed the intensity of the proponents. Packs of business lobbyists buttonholed legislators, decrying the bill. On our side, we had written memos of support from many unions and two comptrollers but no buttonholing. Finally, the bill failed because the attorney general was loath to give up exclusive standing under the Martin Act as it was fighting in New York State appellate courts to preserve even that standing.

The issue isn't just that those with political influence and financial power have some advantages dealing with our government. They are routinely allowed to break the law or operate in gaping holes in the law, with few legal repercussions. Wall Street owns Washington through its huge political contributions and armies of lobbyists. Wall Street has disproportionate influence in Albany and New York City because it is viewed as the "Home Team," whose wrongdoings can be forgiven because to hold it accountable would be to risk wreaking havoc on our New York economy.

For the 2012 legislative session, the Brodsky-Schneiderman bill needed new sponsors. Assemblyman Brodsky did not seek reelection and Senator Schneiderman had moved on to become Attorney General. The Office of the Attorney General did not come out in favor of the Lancman-Libous bill, perhaps because it was litigating the right of the Attorney General to enforce the Martin Act; litigation that ultimately won. The bill itself was substantially the same but was limited to standing for pension funds and not all institutional investors because the groups representing financial institution investors had come out in opposition. The new bill's sponsors were Democratic Assembly Member Rory Lancman of Queens and 26 bipartisan co-sponsors, and Republican Senator Thomas Libous of Binghamton, since the Republicans had won back the majority in the Senate. This bill had mostly the same set of supporters and detractors.

Unfortunately, the New York State Teachers' Retirement System did not join the other public pension funds in supporting the bill. While I never knew why, there was speculation that the bill not being restricted to standing for public pension funds may have been behind the decision to sit it out, despite strong support from the New York State United Teachers board.

Midway through the 2012 session, it became clear to me that this bill would not pass either House. In addition to the strong Wall Street opposition, the Office of the Attorney General did not support the bill because it alters the exclusive jurisdiction of the OAG to enforce the Martin Act. At the suggestion of staff in the Assembly and colleagues in public sector labor, I sought introduction of a new bill that would limit standing to represent the public pension funds under the Martin Act to the Attorney General. The bill provided that when trustees for a public fund asked the Attorney General to investigate a securities fraud case, the Attorney General would be required to do so, and if a settlement or an award were reached, the Attorney General would be required to restitute funds to the affected public pension fund. The bill was introduced on March 22, 2012, in the Assembly by Peter J. Abbate, a Democrat from Brooklyn and Chair of the Government Employees Committee. The bill was later introduced in the Senate by Senator Libous, who also sponsored the (now stuck in legislative mud) Lancman-Libous bill.

The introduction of the Abbate-Libous bill brought pros and cons. The biggest gains were written support from the New York State Association of Counties, representing a bipartisan group of public employers. A second gain was the lessening of opposition from the Office of the Attorney General, since it would now retain its exclusive standing under the Martin Act. On the other hand, the loss of active support from the Office of the New York State Comptroller, which was loath to cede control over litigation involving the Common Retirement Fund to the Office of the Attorney General, was a blow. Private sector unions still supported the Lancman-Libous bill, but public sector union support and focus moved to the Abbate-Libous bill.

But the plot thickens. While all of this legislative maneuvering was going on, the governor, Assembly, and Senate were forging an agreement behind the scenes to cut future public employee pension benefits, and they threw in, for good measure, a partial win for the Martin Act campaign. On March 16, 2012, the so-called Tier 6 Law was enacted to govern most newly hired public employee pensions. This tier included reductions in employee benefits and increases in employee contributions for those benefits. The total savings to public employers in New York State are estimated to be $80 billion over the next 30 years. Spiraling pension obligations have been one of the top financial problems faced by state and local governments across the United States. For New York's municipalities, pension costs have risen more than 650 percent since 2002, so that they were $12.2 billion in 2012. About 40 percent of this increase is attributable to poor investment performance, such as that by New York public funds from 2007–2009. Therefore, the upshot of this poor performance is reduction of employee benefits and increase in employer contributions, even though the damage to the investment performance was caused by neither. Employees and employers suffered in the 2012 solution, but the fraudsters on Wall Street did not suffer at all. There is a straight line between the pension fund asset value losses and the losses to public employees and employers.

There was one ray of light tucked into this Tier 6 pension law that would provide a path to seeking redress against the now well-documented fraudsters: Section 78-a of the bill amended Executive Law 63-c to require the Attorney General to deposit into the public pension fund all monies received in connection with the investigation, commencement, or settlement of an action involving that fund, arising out of its management, operation, investments, or otherwise. This would include all actions commenced under New York's Martin Act. Previously, the statute read that the Attorney General "may" deposit to the fund. This was changed to "shall."

To this day, I do not know how or why this provision was included in the Tier 6 bill. I certainly think that our efforts to expose the asset value losses of the public funds and the lack of adequate statutory redress had something to do with it. No representative of the Governor, Assembly, Senate, Office of the Attorney General, or Trustee of a public fund ever called to say, "Look, we responded to your cries for redress." Usually, someone wants to take credit for a statutory change that might aid public funds in recovering billions of dollars. It has been dead quiet to this day.

Undeterred, and with great excitement, I passed the news of the very significant one-word change along to my public sector union clients and our broad coalition that had lobbied for Martin Act reform. While the enacted solution was half a loaf, if that, at least there was some consolation prize for the public funds for the benefit cuts of Tier 6.

In late 2013, Greg Floyd, President of Local 237 of the Teamsters and a Trustee of the New York City Employees Retirement System, and I approached the Office of the Attorney General (OAG) to find out what arrangements had been made to coordinate between the OAG and the public retirement funds. We were told that no public retirement fund had asked the OAG to start an investigation into any of their '07–'09 asset value injuries. Not only was there not a process in place, but there had been no interest expressed by the public funds. I was perplexed and saddened that our efforts had come to naught, despite the fact that we had actually won a change in the law.

But in Albany, hope springs eternal and things happen when the timing is right. The one-word change from "may" to "shall" could return hundreds of millions to the public pension funds in the future—if attention is paid by the public funds and the Office of the Attorney General. That hasn't happened—yet.

# WORKING STORIES

# BIOGRAPHIES

**Vivian Benton** is the Director of Operations for WDI. She is the former Director of Financial Operations and Analysis at Harvard Medical School.

**Jim Bertolone** has been the President of the American Postal Workers Union since 1990. He was President of the Rochester & Genesee Valley Area Labor Federation (RGVALF).

**Mario Cilento** is President of the New York State AFL-CIO, representing 2.5 million members in the public sector, private sector and building trades.

**Esther Cohen** writes, edits, curates, and teaches. She connects social justice with as many art forms as possible.

**Pat Costello,** a member of IBEW Local 181 and Local 43 for over 35 years, has held every elected position within IBEW's local union structure. Pat is President of Local 43 and has served as the President of the Central New York Labor Council for the past 15 years.

**Rosalie DeFrancesco Drago**, WDI's Long Island regional director, works to forge workforce and economic development collaborations with business, community, and industry.

**Mary Jo Ferrare**, WDI's Mohawk Valley regional director, joined the Laborers' International Union of North America (LIUNA #35) in 1981. She worked as a rank-and-file member, and in 2011, became the first female retiree in the Local's 107-year history.

**Andrea D. Goldberger** is Director of United Food and Commercial Workers (UFCW) Local One Benefit Funds. A lifetime union activist from a union family with long roots, she's Chair of the Board for WDI.

**Susan F. Hains** spent her career in human services in early childhood education. She played a major role in developing the WDI child care initiative. Sue retired in 2015.

**Greg Hart** worked with the Sheet Metal Workers International for 25 years. Today he is the regional director for WDI of the North Country.

**Brian L. Houseal** is an international environmentalist who is now the Director of the Adirondack Ecological Center, SUNY/College of Environmental Science and Forestry.

**Lois Johnson** is the Director of Workforce Strategies for WDI. She is a results-driven workforce professional with over 20 years' executive-level workforce program and policy experience in non-profit and government sectors.

**Richard Lipsitz** is the President of Western New York Area Labor Federation, AFL-CIO. He is a lifelong labor activist.

**Melinda Mack** is the Executive Director of the New York Association of Training and Employment Professionals (NYATEP), a nationally recognized, non-profit membership association. Her focus is promoting, developing, and sustaining the state's workforce system.

**Ed Murphy** is the Director of the Workforce Development Institute. He's a writer, motivational speaker, and reflective practitioner.